ESTABLISHING THE FAMILY-FRIENDLY CAMPUS

Models for Effective Practice

Edited by

Jaime Lester and *Margaret Sallee*

STERLING, VIRGINIA

Sty/us

COPYRIGHT © 2009 BY STYLUS PUBLISHING, LLC.

Published by Stylus Publishing, LLC
22883 Quicksilver Drive
Sterling, Virginia 20166–2102

Library of Congress Cataloging-in-Publication-Data
Establishing the family-friendly campus : models for
effective practice / edited by Jaime Lester and Margaret
Sallee.
        p. cm.
    Includes bibliographical references and index.
    ISBN 978-1-57922-330-4 (hardcover : alk. paper)—
    ISBN 978-1-57922-331-1 (pbk. : alk. paper)
1. College teachers—United States—Leaves of absence.
2. Parental leave—United States.   3. Doctoral
students—Services for—United States.   I. Lester,
Jaime.   II. Sallee, Margaret, 1977–
LB2335.8.E77 2009
378.1'21—dc22   2008054718

13-digit ISBN: 978-1-57922-330-4 (cloth)
13-digit ISBN: 978-1-57922-331-1 (paper)

Printed in the United States of America

All first editions printed on acid free paper
that meets the American National Standards Institute
Z39-48 Standard.

Bulk Purchases

Quantity discounts are available for use in workshops
and for staff development.
Call 1-800-232-0223

First Edition, 2009

10   9   8   7   6   5   4   3   2   1

CONTENTS

PREFACE

Jaime Lester and Margaret Sallee

T his book began many years ago when we, the editors, worked to establish a policy to support graduate students who were experiencing birth or adoption of a child, medical difficulties, or illness in the family (the process of establishing this policy is outlined in Chapter 9). As we worked to create a policy in hopes that a cultural change would follow, we heard many stories from graduate students who were making the difficult choice to support ill family members, take care of their own health problems, postpone having a child, or complete their graduate education. The stories suggested that graduate school and other life circumstances were incompatible. One of the major reasons for the incompatibility was the idiosyncratic ways in which departments and faculty advisors handled the individual students who needed additional accommodation in degree progress, teaching and research assistantships, and extensions for course work. Although some faculty and departments supported students by changing policies and providing exceptional accommodations, others did nothing. The creation of the eventual pregnancy accommodation program helped clarify roles, provide extensions for degree progress, and guarantee funding on return to school. This experience also alerted the editors to the importance of creating policies that begin to chip away at the incompatibility of academe with life.

Graduate students are just the newest population to be incorporated into the work–family balance dialogue. For the past several decades, many institutions in the United States have provided a variety of policies for faculty and staff to help them balance competing responsibilities. Despite their existence, many faculty still struggle to meet multiple expectations. The month before Margaret began graduate school, her first nephew was born. At the time, his father was an assistant professor at a major research institution. As Margaret sat holding her nephew for the first time, she wondered how his father would be able to meet the requirements of tenure and still be an involved parent—

and thought about how she would have the same challenges on becoming an assistant professor herself.

During the writing and editing of this book, Jaime experienced the birth of her first child and confirmed some of Margaret's worries. Although the campus community in which Jaime was teaching was supportive during her pregnancy, she was not offered a structured maternity leave, did not have a department chair who suggested or discussed time off the tenure clock, and was not assisted in finding childcare; rather, Jaime returned to teaching 2 weeks after giving birth because she was concerned that her colleagues did not want "to pick up the slack" and teach her course for the remaining 4 weeks of the semester. Her husband was also not afforded any accommodation because at the time he was a visiting assistant professor, which made him ineligible for any accommodations offered at his institution. Awareness of these issues as assistant professors (which Jaime and her husband certainly had, given the content of this book) is not enough to support faculty, students, and staff who have children, aging parents, and other complex family responsibilities. We all need our institutions of higher education to become aware, accommodating, proactive, and responsible for establishing and supporting family-friendly policies. The goal of this book is to provide a framework, advice, and examples of best practices so that others do not face similar situations when trying to balance work and life.

The Need for Family-Friendly Policies

One of the most important issues in higher education today is the changing workforce. In the last two decades, the demographics of faculty and leaders have shifted from a White male majority to a substantial increase in the numbers of women and people of color. Faculty surveys show an increase in the numbers of women and people of color with small, yet significant, increases in the sciences, which have traditionally been dominated by White men (National Center for Education Statistics, 2005). Although the shift has been less dramatic, student and administrator populations have also changed, and more women and minorities populate administrative roles and college classrooms. The changing population has created a variety of new issues and a demand for policies that address the specific needs of women and people of color.

One of the more prevalent and overarching issues that has gained national attention is the need to develop family-friendly campuses that incorporate a variety of new policies and practices. The increase in the numbers of female faculty has emphasized the need for family leave policies that accommodate childbearing, which often coincides with the tenure clock. Female faculty enter tenure-track faculty positions in their early thirties and must decide whether to forgo childbearing or have a child while trying to achieve tenure. Whereas new faculty are concerned with having children, older faculty face demands at other points in the life cycle. Many of the senior faculty population have elderly parents, thereby leading to a demand for temporary leave and medical insurance for dependents. Furthermore, students are entering higher education at later life stages with family responsibilities that require additional accommodations, such as childcare and dependent insurance. Many graduate students have children while in school and require medical insurance, family and medical leave, and childcare.

The impact of changing demographics in higher education and the importance of family-friendly policies is well documented in the research literature. Female faculty with children leave academe at a disproportionately higher rate than men, have conflicts between academic work and motherhood, and report difficulties in reentering academe after leaving the professoriate (Mason & Goulden, 2004; Ward & Wolf-Wendel, 2004). Female faculty also consistently cite pressure to postpone pregnancy, forgo childbearing to acquire tenure, and hide their pregnancy, refusing to stop the tenure clock for fear of expectations from colleagues regarding productivity (Armenti, 2004). Although many faculty support family-friendly policies such as taking leave following the birth or adoption of a child or stopping the tenure clock, they often do not use these accommodations for fear of suffering career repercussions (Drago et al., 2005; Finkel, Olswang, & She, 1994; Sullivan, Hollenshead, & Smith, 2004; Yoest, 2004). Although we know less about staff and students, accommodations for students and staff with children and aging parents will continue to be an issue on higher education campuses in the future.

The need for more family-friendly policies has not gone unnoticed. Over the past several decades, colleges and universities have implemented a variety of policies to help faculty members balance their personal and professional lives. Though the types of policies available to faculty members vary by institutional type, providing some type of accommodation for new parents is slowly becoming the norm. The University of California (see Chapter 6) has been a leader in providing policies to help faculty members accommodate their competing responsibilities. For example, the university provides one term of paid leave for childbearing mothers, up to two terms (either quarters or semesters, depending on the campus) of a reduction of teaching duties without a reduction in pay, and the opportunity to stop the tenure clock for 1 year. Princeton University recently gained national attention by implementing a mandatory 1-year stoppage of the tenure clock for every faculty member—male or female—who welcomes a new child into his or her family. Furthermore, foundations, such as the Alfred P. Sloan Foundation in partnership with the American Council on Education (see Chapter 1) have developed specific programs to provide funding for universities to develop policies and practices that create family-friendly campuses for faculty.

Faculty are not the only campus members who benefit from family-friendly policies. Many campuses offer a variety of services and leave policies that staff members can use. Graduate students have become the newest constituents to have access to policies. In the past several years, major research institutions including MIT, Stanford, and the University of Southern California have implemented policies to provide paid leave and other accommodations to pregnant graduate students. Family medical leave policies, lactation rooms, and dependent medical benefits are common on many campuses, including the University of Michigan, The Ohio State University, and the University of Washington. Although not all institutions offer a range of policies for faculty and staff, most provide at least some accommodations to help employees achieve a balance between their personal and professional lives.

Documenting Best Practices

Although the past decade has seen a rise in policy changes and scholarly literature that explores the challenges that faculty face in balancing their competing responsibilities, equal attention has not been given to the most effective or the "best" practices and the nature of those practices. Furthermore, public attention and research has primarily ignored the need for and scope of family-friendly policies for students and administrators in higher education. Most of the current practices are being developed in isolation, with little evidence of their effectiveness. In this book, we examine the need for family-friendly policies and document the best practices currently being implemented to create more family-friendly campus environments. Each chapter describes policies available at institutions around the country and provides suggestions for implementation for interested administrators, faculty, and students.

Chapter 1, written by Gloria Thomas and Jean McLaughlin based on their work at the American Council on Education (ACE), begins with an introduction of the Alfred P. Sloan Awards for Faculty Career Flexibility established in partnership with ACE. Thomas and McLaughlin describe several outstanding models of faculty career flexibility policies and programs and outline important issues to consider to successfully create faculty career flexibility initiatives on any college or university campus. Many of the best practices outlined in the subsequent chapters were funded through the Sloan grants.

Chapter 2 focuses on the work–life balance efforts at the University of Washington. Kate Quinn and Randi Shapiro highlight some of UW's best practices—flexible work arrangements (FWAs), childcare, and emergency supports—with a focus on strategies for duplicating these programs at other institutions.

Chapter 3 continues the discussion of institutional specific programs with a focus on the innovative UA Life & Work Connections (LWC) program at the University of Arizona. Caryn Jung, David Swihart, and Darci Thompson describe how LWC, the designated work–life unit for faculty and staff, developed the social ecology of health model that serves as the foundation for all of the office's programming, and how the hybrid design allows for timely responses throughout the campus environment.

In Chapter 4, Jill Bickett and Emily Arms turn the focus from research institutions to medium-sized Catholic universities. They suggest that the Jesuit mission, with a focus on respect for the whole individual, provides a natural opening for the provision of family-friendly policies. As their review of six such institutions suggests, most provide some sort of assistance to faculty and staff, though none have the resources to provide aid similar to research institutions.

Chapter 5, the final chapter that discusses the family-friendly policies at specific universities, highlights the history of the Office of WORKlife Programs at the Johns Hopkins Institutions (JHI) in Baltimore, Maryland.

Using John Kotter's (1995) eight steps for organizational change, Kathleen Beauchesne describes the changes that the institution underwent to create a culture that recognized the need to help faculty and staff balance their personal and professional responsibilities.

Whereas other chapters in this book have described specific practices at either individual or a group of institutions, the next set of chapters outline ways to create change by and for specific populations, principally department chairs, deans, faculty, and graduate students. In Chapter 6, Karie Frasch, Angelica Stacy, Mary Ann Mason, Sharon Page-Medrich, and Marc Goulden discuss the groundbreaking family-friendly policies at the University of California. Rather than focus on specific policies, however, the authors outline how department chairs can create cultural change within individual academic departments. Specific recommendations include making the use of family accommodations the standard for conducting business, maintaining zero tolerance for discriminatory and disparaging comments and behaviors, implementing small changes that can have a significant impact on departmental culture, and assessing the effectiveness of efforts toward family friendliness.

Chapter 7, by Sharon McDade and Sharon Dannels, provides a unique account of the academic medicine and dentistry dean's perspective of family-friendly policies and work climate. Deans are a particularly important group because they play an important role in advancing the faculty work environment. Using data from the Executive Leadership in Academic Medicine Program for Women (ELAM) study, McDade and Dannels illustrate perceptions of work climate and adoption of family-friendly policies over time.

In Chapter 8, Jeni Hart shares the specific ways in which faculty in two grassroots faculty organizations pursued a family-friendly agenda. These groups used two distinctive strategies for change; their efforts illustrate how faculty can promote a family-friendly agenda throughout their institutions. This chapter is helpful for faculty who are interested in pursuing family-friendly policies within their academic communities.

Chapter 9, by Margaret Sallee, Mariko Dawson Zare, and Jaime Lester, who were all once graduate students at the University of Southern California, describes the process of creating a pregnancy accommodation program, lactation rooms, and a support network for graduate student parents. Given graduate students' lack of financial resources, the fact that they are not considered employees and therefore not eligible for the same accommodations as faculty and staff, and the fact that they often enroll in master's and doctoral programs during peak childbearing years, establishing family-friendly policies is particularly important for this population. This chapter concludes with several recommendations for graduate students and administrators who are interested in establishing these policies for graduate students.

The final chapter of this book, Chapter 10, reflects on the history of work–family balance before considering necessary changes to the definition of the family-friendly campus. Using Rosalind Barnett's (1999) work as a guide, Margaret Sallee and Jaime Lester suggest that the most effective campuses are those that use a work–life systems framework to meet the needs of their employees. They also point to future growth areas for the family-friendly campus, including expanding the focus from faculty and staff to incorporate all in the campus community; expanding to new institutional types, such as the community college; and introducing new types of policies.

References

Armenti, C. (2004). May babies and posttenure babies: Maternal decisions of women professors. *The Review of Higher Education, 27*(2), 211–231.

Barnett, R. C. (1999). A new work-life model for the twenty-first century. *Annals of the American Academy of Political and Social Science, 562,* 143–158.

Drago, R., Colbeck, C., Stauffer, K. D., Pirretti, A., Burkum, K., Fazioli, J., et al. (2005). Bias against caregiving. *Academe, 91*(5), 22–25.

Finkel, S. K., Olswang, S., & She, N. (1994). Childbirth, tenure, and promotion for women faculty. *The Review of Higher Education, 17*(3), 259–270.

Kotter, J. P. (1995). Leading change: Why transformation efforts fail. Harvard Business Review. Reprint R0701. Retrieved March 15, 2008 from http://www.hbrreprints.org

Mason, M. A., & Goulden, M. (2004). Do babies matter (Part II)? Closing the baby gap. *Academe, 90*(6), 10–15.

National Center for Education Statistics. (2005). 2004 National Study of Postsecondary Faculty (NSOPF:04). Report on Faculty and Instructional Staff in Fall 2003. (NCES 2005–172). Washington, DC: U.S. Department of Education, Institute of Educational Sciences.

Sullivan, B., Hollenshead, C., & Smith, G. (2004). Developing and implementing work-family policies for faculty. *Academe, 90*(6), 24–27.

Ward, K., & Wolf-Wendel, L. (2004). Fear factor: How safe is it to make time for family? *Academe, 90*(6), 28–31.

Yoest, C. (2004, February). *Parental leave in academia.* Retrieved November 9, 2004, from http://www.faculty.virginia.edu/familyandtenure/

CHALLENGES AND EFFORTS OF CAREER FLEXIBILITY IN HIGHER EDUCATION

Gloria D. Thomas and Jean M. McLaughlin

Faculty career flexibility is a term used in academia to describe policies and practices that address concerns related to work–life issues for faculty. At the American Council on Education (ACE), our concern for flexibility in the academy stems from the dire need to keep Ph.D.s in the higher education sector and to use institutional policies to recruit talented scholars into academia and retain them over the course of their academic careers. Faculty members often stay at one institution for their whole academic lives; they also often stay within higher education for their entire careers. Therefore, investing in faculty to retain them in the academy makes sense for institutions across the postsecondary sector. In this chapter, we provide our definition of faculty career flexibility, review the trends from the Alfred P. Sloan Awards for Faculty Career Flexibility, and describe several outstanding models of faculty career flexibility policies and programs that can be replicated. Finally, we share requisite keys to building successful faculty career flexibility initiatives on any college or university campus.

Faculty Career Flexibility: Definitions, Descriptions, and Rationale

Stemming from a 2005 ACE and Alfred P. Sloan Foundation collaboration, we originally defined faculty career flexibility as *a strategic tool to realign the structure of the career path to the needs of the academic workforce.* After working directly with institutions, both winners and others interested in expanding choices for faculty career options, we have added more components to this working definition. Here we present our definitions used for the awards process and the brief literature review supporting the rationale for flexibility in the academy.

Definitions and Descriptions

For the purposes of the awards process, broad models of career flexibility policies and practices were framed under one of the following categories: tenure clock adjustment (e.g., stopping the tenure clock for childbirth or other critical life events, or applying earlier for tenure); active service modified duties (ASMD), temporary relief, or modification/reduction in duties (e.g., reduced teaching, research, or service duties for a temporary amount of time, usually at full pay); on- and off-ramps (e.g., through leave policies, such as extended family and medical leave for childbirth, adoption, or elder care, or disability leave); temporary part-time appointments (e.g., allowing mobility between a full-time and part-time appointment for a designated period of time); phased retirement (e.g., reduced or part-time appointments for finite periods of time leading up to retirement); and delayed entry (e.g., hiring a Ph.D. into a tenure-track line after previous employment in another industry or a non-tenure-track position in academia).

Since establishing this definition and framework, ACE has come to realize just how critical dependent care (i.e., children, sick family/friend/partner, and/or elders) and dual-career appointments are in the composition of a comprehensive package of flexible career policies and practices for recruiting, retaining, and retiring tenure-track and tenured faculty. Several of the best practices presented in this chapter address these issues as well. Next, we present the rationale for the urgent need to have faculty career flexibility policies and practices in place.

Why the Need for Faculty Career Flexibility Now?

One of the first products generated from partnership between ACE and the Sloan Foundation to advance faculty career flexibility in U.S. higher education was the publication of a groundbreaking report, *An Agenda for Excellence: Creating Flexibility in Tenure-Track Faculty Careers.* Endorsed by a national panel of presidents and chancellors from major research universities across the country, this publication was the first national call for institutional leaders to implement recommended flexible career policies and practices. Flexibility in the academy can be critical to help U.S. higher education remain competitive internationally by attracting and keeping the most talented tenured and tenure-track faculty. The report outlined how flexible career policies and practices may be used to address the need to proactively examine and transform institutional structures that prevent talented scholars from entering, thriving in, and retiring from academia with dignity and financial security (American Council on Education, 2005, p. v).

A unique opportunity has presented itself for institutional structural changes as a result of the record-breaking retirements among baby boomer faculty as well as the tremendous growth in student enrollments nationally. Because of these occurrences, higher education institutions are encountering unprecedented increases in new tenure-track faculty hires since the 1970s (Broad, 2005; Brown, 2005). As the demographics of the academic workforce shift (i.e., from a mostly White male professoriate to a more diverse, younger generation of male and female faculty who come from various racial/ethnic and socioeconomic backgrounds), so too must the structure and rigidity of their career paths be altered to accommodate the changes these new faculty bring to the academy.

Other studies and publications echo the acute need for faculty career flexibility because the American professoriate is no longer composed solely of "ideal workers." When baby boomers and the generation before them were hired into academia, most faculty were White males whose personal lives did not supersede professional responsibilities because they had wives who stayed home to attend to personal affairs such as caring for the children and managing the household (Bailyn, 1993; Williams, 1999). With the dramatic increase in the number of women, faculty of color, single parents, and even men who enter tenured and tenure-track faculty positions demanding greater flexibility in their personal and professional responsibilities, flexible policies and practices are needed now more than ever. Female faculty, in particular, need the flexibility in their professional spheres, as they still shoulder a great majority of dependent-care responsibilities while striving to give due diligence to their research, teaching, and service responsibilities (Gmelch, Willse, & Lourich, 1986; Mason & Goulden, 2002; Mason & Goulden, 2004; Williams, 2000). Women are also severely disadvantaged by the rigidity of the faculty career path, if they are interested in having children, as the tenure path collides with peak fertility years. Thus, family planning becomes a career-threatening proposition, which is rarely a consideration for most male faculty (Marcus, 2007).

Because women are less likely to enjoy career success at the same rates and levels as men (i.e., with respect to rank, research productivity, prestige of institution, and retention in career), Judith Glazer (1997) argues for the need for alternative models in the academic structure as a result of the accumulative disadvantages experienced by women. Glazer suggests that institutional leaders examine not why women are incompatible with the professoriate, but why academic career structures are more compatible with men. Furthermore, it is not sufficient to have policies and programs in place if, as studies show, faculty avoid using available flexibility policies for fear of reprisal (Drago et al., 2006). In responding to these calls for institutional change in academia, the Sloan Foundation, through its Workplace, Work Force and Working Families Program, has seized the opportunity to support the overhaul of the structural mismatch between academia and the current tenured and tenure-track workforce.

The Alfred P. Sloan Foundation's Awards for Faculty Career Flexibility

The Sloan Foundation has committed itself, through the programs and research funded by program director Kathleen Christensen, to abate the "workplace/workforce mismatch" that exists in most industries—including academia. One of the ideas that emerged from the collaborative efforts between ACE and the Sloan Foundation was to create an awards program to identify institutions leading the way in flexible career policy implementation for tenured and tenure-track faculty, thereby creating models for other institutions to replicate. Along with earning distinction as a leader for policies and practices in faculty career flexibility, winning institutions would also receive a generous monetary award to accelerate the awareness and use of existing policies by faculty. The goal of these awards was to publicly broadcast the winners and their accomplishments to serve as replicable models for reshaping the cultural infrastructure of academic departments, especially through best practices in encouraging and advocating for the use of flexible faculty career policies and practices without career penalties.

The project team for the Sloan Awards decided that the first round of Alfred P. Sloan Awards for Faculty Career Flexibility would be open to all 259 doctoral/research extensive and intensive universities, as was defined by the then-current 2000 Carnegie Classification system. This decision was based on the anecdotal belief that these institutions were more likely to have flexible career policies and practices in place than other institutional types. A subsequent study funded by the Sloan Foundation and conducted by the Center for the Education of Women at the University of Michigan confirmed that doctoral/research universities have the highest number of policies among all institutional types (Center for the Education of Women, 2005).

Trends That Emerged From the Institutional Questionnaire

Among the 55 institutions that applied for the Sloan Awards for Faculty Career Flexibility, several trends emerged for policies and practices that the institutions indicated were already in place. Specifically, we asked about adjusting or stopping the tenure clock, partial relief from duties or modified/reduced duties, paid and unpaid leaves with no professional obligations to the institution, part-time appointments, phased retirement, institutional culture supporting flexibility, and institutional goals. Responses to the Institutional Questionnaire indicated that nearly two-thirds or more of the applicants had the following written, university-wide policies in place:

- Temporary relief from or a reduction in teaching or other duties for family care and/or personal disability with no reduction in pay for both tenured and tenure-track faculty (78% of institutions)
- Tenure clock stop for tenure-track faculty under certain circumstances (96%); 64% of institutions track the use of tenure clock stop in relation to tenure outcomes
- Full paid leave for tenured or tenure-track female faculty who are new biological mothers during the period of disability related to pregnancy and childbirth (76%)

Approximately half of the applicant institutions also had these generous policies in place:

- Full paid leave for tenured and tenure-track new biological mothers *after* the period of disability (55%)

- Formal written policies allowing part-time appointments for tenured and tenure-track faculty (49%)
- Formal written policies allowing phased retirement (49%); most of the institutions that allow phased retirement continue to contribute to the faculty member's retirement benefits on a prorated basis (56%) or as if the faculty member were working full time (an additional 26%)

Policies and practices such as having special funds held in the central university administration (i.e., provost's office) to temporarily hire replacement instructors for faculty on leave from the classroom; written policies determining workload for faculty who use temporary relief or modified/reduced duties; temporary part-time appointments for tenure-track faculty for a fixed period of time; and tracking the use and outcomes of policies were rare at the applicant universities.

Awards for Leading Efforts: The Winners

The five winners of the 2006 Sloan Awards were Duke University, Lehigh University, the University of California (Berkeley and Davis campuses), the University of Florida, and the University of Washington. Two additional institutions received $25,000 awards each for their innovative practices in career flexibility: Iowa State University, for creating a database and tracking system to quantify the benefits that can accrue from flexible career policies and to conduct a cost-benefit analysis of these policies, particularly as they relate to faculty career decisions and productivity; and the University of Wisconsin, Madison, for its Vilas Life Cycle Professorship program, which provides financial support and personal attention to faculty who encounter critical junctures in their careers that affect both their research and their personal lives.

Selected Highlights from the Winning Research Universities

In determining the winners of the Alfred P. Sloan Awards, the judges considered institutional commitment, tracking and measuring performance, sustainability, and innovative policies and programs. However, the judges also recognized that each institution would have unique plans to accommodate the faculty needs on its campus. The following are selected innovative policies and/or practices from the initiatives of the winning institutions to accelerate faculty career flexibility on their respective campuses.

Implementing a Strategic Awareness Campaign

The 10 campuses within the University of California (UC) System had some of the most comprehensive flexibility and family-friendly policies in place before the offering of the Sloan Awards. However, noting historical low usage, the objectives of UC Berkeley and Davis were to ensure that all current and incoming faculty know about available policies and resources, and that administrators and those involved in the merit/review process understand their responsibilities for supporting faculty. Thus, the efforts at UC Berkeley and Davis, which were led by a team of senior administrators, researchers, and human resources managers, focused primarily on creating greater awareness of existing policies and practices already in place; tracking and evaluating outcomes of policy use and participation in flexibility programs and practices; monitoring and tracking all requests to prevent policy abuse; and most important, disseminating their best practices and accomplishments to all 10 of the UC campuses for implementation systemwide. These educational efforts can be seen on the UC Faculty Family Friendly Edge Web pages (http://ucfamilyedge.berkeley.edu/ucfamilyfriendlyedge.html).

A Model for Flexible Work Arrangements (FWA)

In its accelerator plan, Duke outlined the goal of providing flexible work arrangements for faculty university-wide, including the School of Medicine. Through this flexible work arrangements (FWA) policy, passed by the Academic Council and the Board of Trustees in May 2007, faculty are allowed to modify their work schedules with approval from the department chair and/or dean in order to ensure the ability of a school or department to carry out its mission and duties. Although other applicant institutions for the Sloan Awards reported that they allow at least one semester, quarter, or term of temporary relief from or reduction of professional duties, few reported generous policies like Duke's FWA, which can be arranged for up to 3 years and, under certain circumstances, can be renewed for additional terms. With approval from the dean and/or chair, the faculty member may choose which duties to reduce. Tenure-track faculty are automatically eligible for 3 months of tenure clock relief for each year of FWA (with an overall 3-year limit of tenure clock extensions).

Measuring Usage and Tracking Outcomes

All of the winning institutions were expected to track faculty use of flexible career policies and monitor outcomes over the 2-year period in which ACE was involved with this project. Preliminary data from some of the institutions suggest an increase in the use of policies since the beginning of the Sloan Award period. However, most institutions have used tracking to establish baseline data. Some examples of the type of data tracked and collected include the number of Duke faculty granted use of the tenure clock stop policy and the number of parental leaves approved. The two UC campuses have tracked the cost of replacement instructors for faculty on childbearing leave or ASMD. The University of Florida has tracked the number of agreements of support for placements of spouses and domestic partners through its Dual Career Services program either within or outside the University.

The University of Washington (UW) has collected data for deans and department chairs to mark and compare progress in hiring, promoting, and other measures of faculty success. The Office of the Provost for Academic Personnel publishes a fact sheet with statistics on faculty by rank; new hires by rank and year; and numbers of promotions, resignations, and faculty who use leave policies by school, college, and campus. In addition to these data on the status of faculty, UW has also begun tracking the use of tenure clock extensions (TCE), including reasons why faculty have used this policy, analyzed by field, gender, and race.

Eliminating Bias for Using Flexible Career Options

To address bias against underrepresented groups (e.g., women and people of color) in the faculty search and hiring process, the University of Florida developed a mandatory training session for all search committee members. Part of the online training addresses biases toward nontraditional candidates (those with delayed entry into tenure-track positions, racial/ethnic minorities, gay or lesbian candidates, etc.) or toward candidates who are part of a dual-career couple. Certificates, good for 3 years, indicating completion of a university-sponsored recruitment tutorial or workshop have been required since the fall of 2007 for all search committee members on appointment and before participating in a search.

To help eliminate penalties in the promotion and tenure process against faculty who take advantage of flexible career policies, UC Davis coordinates across the 10 UC campuses the sharing of internal and external sample letters for review committees, including examples of family accommodation policy use and instructions regarding evaluation for promotion and tenure without prejudice.

Rewarding Usage

Lehigh has developed an innovative practice of rewarding faculty who take advantage of its Family and Medical Leave policy; it automatically provides $6,000 grants to all tenure-track faculty who take leave to care for a family member. The purpose of the grant is to help the faculty member maintain visibility in his or her department and at disciplinary conferences during the leave and to assist in the transition back to full-time status. The grants have been used for computer purchases and other research-related expenses as well as family care and housekeeping, which disproportionately take up female faculty members' time away from research as they transition back from family leave. The provost and deans have agreed to share the cost of continuing this program beyond the Sloan Award period. During the 2006–2007 academic year, eight of the nine eligible faculty completed the paper work to receive one of the research grants.

Preventing Misuse

Evaluating the proper use of flexibility policies is critical to deflect detractors' concerns about misuse. To avoid faculty exploiting the use of policies that were implemented to aid recruitment and retention, UC Berkeley began investigating faculty abuse of flexible career policy use—particularly ASMD, tenure clock extensions, and part-time appointments—as a means to determine how best to ensure equitable use. The main concern is that some faculty, particularly those who are new parents but not "substantial caregivers," may use these policies to provide extra time to increase their research activities. This could lead to an unfair advantage and may eventually cause amplification of tenure expectations. The practice that has been implemented to help stem the tide on policy abuse is to negotiate a Memorandum of Understanding (MOU) for the individual faculty member requesting use of the part-time policy, with input and approval from the department chair and dean. Faculty requesting to use other family accommodation policies must indicate that they are a substantial caregiver—that is, that they perform 50% or more of childcare duties.

Funding

The cost of implementing and providing faculty career flexibility policies and programs is often cited as one of the challenges to doing so. Iowa State University (ISU), which won one of the two Innovative Practice Awards, has developed a model database and tracking system to quantify the benefits that can accrue from flexible career policies. It has started conducting a cost-benefit analysis of these policies, particularly as they relate to faculty career decisions and productivity. In California, the UC campuses have removed financial disincentives at the department and school/college level for encouraging flexibility. UC Davis has promoted its model of central funding for replacement teaching costs for faculty on childbearing leave or ASMD to all 10 UC campuses.

Unanticipated but Common Problems Addressed in Accelerator Plans

The institutions that completed accelerator plans all had a unique set of goals to advance the recruitment, retention, and retirement of talented scholars. In addition to their individual institutional pursuits, two common problems that were consistently noted in the plans were the need to better accommodate dual-career couples and childcare for faculty. Here, we briefly describe two practices implemented at the winning research universities to address these unanticipated but common problems.

Dual-Career Couples

All of the winning universities were challenged to varying degrees with job placements for spouses/partners of dual-career couples. Most of them addressed the dual-career couple dilemma similarly by relying on existing resources and coordinating with their neighboring institutions to help place spouses/partners in professional positions in or outside the university. Most have adopted the "one-third policy" for placing spouses/partners—that is, spouses/partners are hired, usually on a trial basis; for the first 3 years the university pays $1/3$ of the spouse/partner's salary from a centralized fund from the provost's office; the provost at the external university (placement institution) pays $\frac{1}{3}$; and the hiring department (also at the placement institution) pays $\frac{1}{3}$. Most of the universities also have similar internal processes for hiring and compensating spouses/partners in which the offices of the provost, dean, and department chair each contribute $\frac{1}{3}$ of the spouse/partner's salary. Because of its relative isolation, Lehigh University used part of its Sloan grant to expand its placement options by joining the nearest chapter of the national Higher Education Recruitment Consortium (HERC), which now has become the New Jersey–Eastern Pennsylvania chapter. In addition to these offerings, some of the institutions decided to make the services of their respective campus career offices available to spouses/partners seeking employment.

Childcare

Providing more quality and affordable childcare was the other common challenge for most of the campuses. As Kate Quinn and Randi Shapiro detail in Chapter 2, the need for infant care is a critical problem at the University of Washington. The available slots in quality childcare centers in Seattle are financially out of reach for many faculty and are quickly reserved by employees from more lucrative area technology and biomedical corporations. Using funding provided by its Sloan grant, the University of Washington has developed a comprehensive approach to tackling this problem. It has secured funding to supplement the cost of childcare for faculty and purchased childcare slots at existing childcare centers that can be used as incentives for new faculty recruits.

Challenges in the Implementation of the Sloan Award Initiatives

Institutions met a number of challenges in implementing their accelerator plans. Public institutions were more likely to meet additional challenges than their private counterparts because of state laws that would prohibit change— nevertheless, all encountered obstacles to varying degrees. Without identifying the institutions in conjunction with these challenges, we note some of the greatest stumbling blocks experienced.

The Need to Achieve Buy-In From Key Campus Constituents

At one of the winning institutions, the human resources leader was not fully on board with the accelerator plan or how and why it was to be implemented. This resulted in a major communication gap between key stakeholders and leaders and ultimately affected the institution's level of success in meeting its stated goals and objectives for advancing faculty career flexibility. The lesson learned is to have the broadest possible input in the development of the accelerator plan and buy-in from as many relevant constituents as possible before pursuing a set of goals. Establishing this broad-based foundation for the common desire and approach to advance faculty career flexibility, especially among faculty and key administrative leaders, is time consuming but essential for successful results.

Prioritizing Budgets

One institution experienced severe state budget cuts that resulted in an institutional hiring freeze, faculty line reductions, and some layoffs. In light of this budget crunch in which some personnel lost their livelihoods, it was difficult to justify making faculty career flexibility among the highest institutional priorities, given other pressing concerns. The lesson learned in this case is to view faculty career flexibility as a critical tool for recruiting and retaining talented faculty for the coveted positions that exist at the institution. If faculty career flexibility policies and practices such as sabbatical leaves become a part of standard operating procedures, few will question their relevance and importance.

Striving to Make Changes Deep and Pervasive

Another institution discontinued one of its career flexibility initiatives developed in the accelerator plan. This program was targeted specifically to new mothers. Participation was low and inconsistent, and female faculty did not always feel that their participation was worthwhile. The lesson learned is to be sure that new initiatives that are designed to promote institutional structural change are deep and pervasive, and thus sustainable. In an ideal situation, new policies and practices should apply to all faculty in order to be pervasive and far-reaching. The depth of policies and practices is high when there is a strong likelihood of faculty using them. Thus, new initiatives should address the needs of the faculty in a manner that allows the policies and practices to transform the culture of how work is conducted at the institution.

Restrictions of State and Religious Laws

Another institutional challenge that is specific to state and religiously affili-ated institutions occurs when policies and laws prohibit or conflict with the proposed change initiative. Not only was this an issue for the winning insti-tutions, but many have found it a general challenge when striving to adopt policies regarding benefits for faculty who are employed less than full time, in the case of state institutions (including phasing into retirement) and fac-ulty with same-sex partners in the case of both state and some religious insti-tutions. The lesson learned for state institutions is to identify the constituent groups who need to be brought into the discussions early on for their input and buy-in for new policies and practices related to recruiting and maintain-ing a competitive workforce in the state's colleges and universities. In the case of religious institutions, other accommodation policies and practices that benefit faculty recruitment and retention could make up for those that are prohibited by religious order. For example, a Catholic college may not be able to offer health insurance to same-sex partners but it may be able to provide a cafeteria-style health care and dependent-care benefits plan that could alternatively benefit same-sex or unmarried couples.

Some Institutional Challenges for Faculty Career Flexibility Policies and Practices

In some fields, particularly science, technology, engineering, and mathemat-ics (STEM) as well as business, taking time off can threaten funding for research. In these fields, funding continuity and institutional culture drive faculty to forgo taking advantage of leaves and extensions. Most foundations and grant agencies typically do not allow for tenure clock stops and exten-sions of grants either. In addition to institutional changes, funding agencies must accommodate career flexibility too.

Other challenges persist with particular policies such as part-time appointments. When a tenure-track or tenured faculty goes part time, insti-tutions find it challenging to ensure that funds are preserved to let him or her come back to a full-time appointment later. Similarly, institutions are finding it difficult to determine how to evaluate dossiers fairly for faculty working less than full time. UC Berkeley has been working on the details of how to implement the part-time policy in an equitable and productive manner. It has begun the process by collecting and sharing sample MOUs previously negotiated that can be used in different situations, such as temporary shifts to part-time status, permanent shifts to part-time status, and shifts from part-time to full-time status. As faculty across the campus begin to use the part-time option more, leaders will carefully track short- and long-term effects of part-time appointments for tenure-track and tenured faculty on faculty careers. Because few tenured and tenure-track faculty currently take advantage of the part-time policy, this examination will continue to take place over time.

In publicizing policies and programs, a clear connection should exist between how faculty career flexibility policies and practices help advance institutional goals to promote excellence, not lower standards. Faculty career flexibility policies and practices need to be projected and viewed by all faculty as critical tools for meeting work–life satisfaction, not just a perk for faculty who choose to have children. The winning institutions have focused their attention on buy-in from all constituents by publicizing faculty career flexibility policies, practices, and programs as needed benefits to all faculty across the life span of their careers—from entry to retirement. Thus, these institutions have worked to avoid the stigma associated with use.

Key Strategies for Building Successful Faculty Career Flexibility Initiatives

Two key strategies proved useful in sustaining faculty career flexibility initiatives on campus: leadership from the top and accountability of academic affairs administrators, who are partially responsible for promoting the fair and equitable use of flexibility initiatives.

Leadership from the Top

Through our work with the winning research universities and other institutions, ACE has found that the most critical component to successful implementation, use, and evaluation of faculty career flexibility policies and practices is the support of the president and chief academic officer. Top institutional leaders must view faculty career flexibility as a necessary tool to advance recruitment and retention of valued scholars in order for deans, department chairs, faculty senate leaders, and the wider faculty body to lend their buy-in and support. Leadership from the top was especially evident at Lehigh University as the institution underwent a transition in presidential leadership during the application process. In spite of this change, nothing interfered with the institution's ability to successfully compete and meet its intended goals in advancing career flexibility policies and practices. This achievement can be attributed, in large part, to the provost's steadfast commitment to this project, in addition to the new president's strong advocacy for flexible career options as tools for recruiting and retaining talented faculty.

Accountability

Accountability measures must also be put in place when implementing new policies or encouraging the use of existing policies and practices. Deans, department chairs, and directors first need to be aware of the package of available policies and practices in order to encourage their use. Consideration should be given to how these leaders can be rewarded through job performance and review for merit increases as well as college budget reviews for successfully educating faculty about, and when necessary, encouraging faculty to use flexible faculty career policies and practices. As a means of broadening acceptance of career flexibility, the University of Florida (UF) started measuring accountability for deans, department chairs, and directors to encourage the use of and manage flexible faculty career policies and practices through job performance and college budget reviews. In tandem with accountability, UF also implemented an awards program for department and unit leaders who make notable strides to encourage an atmosphere of acceptance for career flexibility accommodations.

Conclusion

The overarching goal of the Sloan Awards was to get institutions to accelerate and sustain flexible career policies and practices, and we are pleased to see the important flexible career initiatives that the winning universities will sustain. All of the winning institutions have made a commitment to continue with the most successful policies and practices that they developed during the 2-year Sloan Awards period, including Duke's new flexible work arrangements policy, Lehigh's rewarding faculty for using family medical leave, UC

Berkeley and Davis's flexible career awareness campaign, the University of Florida's online search committee training and certification, and the University of Washington's initiatives to increase quality childcare slots for faculty. If the implementation, use, and evaluation of faculty career flexibility policies and practices are not made institutional priorities, then these initiatives will not be sustainable. The examples presented in this chapter demonstrate best practices in faculty career flexibility that can be replicated on almost any college or university campus.

References

American Council on Education. (2005). *An agenda for excellence: Creating flexibility in tenure-track faculty careers.* Washington, DC: Author.

Bailyn, L. (1993). *Breaking the mold: Women, men, and time in the new corporate world.* New York: Free Press.

Broad, M. C. (2005). Filling the gap: Finding and keeping faculty for the university of the future. In R. L. Clark & J. Ma (Eds.), *Recruitment, retention, and retirement in higher education—building and managing the faculty of the future.* Conference Volume: TIAA-CREF Institute Series on Higher Education. Northhampton, MA: Elgar.

Brown, B. E. (2005, November 10). Report to the Personnel and Tenure Committee, UNC Board of Governors: UNC Phased Retirement Program. Retrieved March 7, 2008, from http://www.northcarolina.edu/content.php/aa/reports/planned_retirement/index.htm

Center for the Education of Women. (2005). *Family-friendly policies in higher education: Where do we stand?* Ann Arbor: University of Michigan.

Drago, R., Colbeck, C. L., Stauffer, K. D., Pirretti, A., Burkum, K., Fazioli, J., et al. (2006). The avoidance of bias against caregiving. *American Behavioral Scientist, 49*(9), 1222–1247.

Glazer, J. S. (1997). Affirmative action and the status of women in the academy. In C. Marshall (Ed.), *Feminist critical policy analysis: A perspective from postsecondary education* (pp. 60–73). London: Falmer Press.

Gmelch, W. H., Willse, P. K., & Lourich, N. P. (1986). Dimensions of stress among university faculty: Factor analytic results from a national study. *Research in Higher Education, 24,* 266–285.

Marcus, J. (2007, March/April). Helping academics have families and tenure too. *Change, 39*(2), 27–32.

Mason, M. A., & Goulden, M. (2002). Do babies matter? The effect of family formation on the lifelong careers of academic men and women. *Academe, 88*(6), 21–27.

Mason, M. A., & Goulden, M. (2004). Do babies matter (Part II)? Closing the baby gap. *Academe, 90*(6), 10–15.

Williams, J. (1999). *Unbending gender: Why family and work conflict and what to do about it.* New York: Oxford University Press.

Williams, J. (2000, December 15). What stymies women's academic careers? It's personal. *Chronicle of Higher Education,* p. B10.

2

BALANCE@UW

Work–Family Cultural Change at the University of Washington

Kate Quinn and Randi Shapiro

The Balance@UW initiative began in 2006 when the University of Washington (UW) won one of five Alfred P. Sloan Awards for Faculty Career Flexibility in recognition of efforts to improve work–life conditions for faculty. Specific goals include piloting new programs and policies to support faculty parents, increasing the availability of childcare for faculty, and working toward work–family cultural change. Balance@UW is the culmination of decades of effort to support the work–life balance of faculty, staff, and students, including program development and cultural change initiatives. Various flexible policy options and family-friendly supports have been implemented over the past 30 years. These supports provide a variety of options across the life and career course, including flexibility in work structures for faculty and staff, lactation stations, parenting seminars, elder care support groups, on-site childcare facilities, and childcare vouchers for students.

UW is not alone in efforts to support caregivers. A growing body of literature indicates that many institutions are attempting to create supportive environments (see, e.g., Blackburn & Hollenshead, 1999; Massachusetts Institute of Technology [MIT], 1999). Researchers have examined topics such as the availability of flexible policy options for faculty (Drago & Colbeck, 2003; Friedman, Rimsky, & Johnson, 1996; Raabe, 1997); faculty workload and work–life satisfaction (Gappa & MacDermid, 1997; Hensel,

1991; Jacobs & Winslow, 2004); faculty decisions to start families (Mason & Goulden, 2002); and how faculty balance multiple roles (Wolf-Wendel & Ward, 2006). The American Council on Education (2005) and the Committee on Maximizing the Potential of Women in Academic Science and Engineering (2006) have called for increasing the flexibility of faculty careers to improve gender equity and the ability of American institutions of higher education to compete in a global market. As more members of Generation X and Generation Y enter the faculty ranks, work–life flexibility for faculty will become even more important (Bickel & Brown, 2005; Lancaster & Stillman, 2003).

This chapter highlights some of UW's best practices for implementing inclusive supports and working toward work–family cultural change and offers tips for replication. UW's best practices fall within three broad categories: flexible work arrangements (FWAs), childcare, and emergency supports. Within each category, we detail UW's best practices for faculty and staff. First, we introduce the University of Washington and its history of work–family efforts.

Context and History

The University of Washington is a public research university that was founded in 1861. It has been a member of the Association of American Universities since 1950. As of 2007, UW had approximately 27,800 faculty and staff and 43,000 students. In fiscal year 2007, UW received more than $1 billion in gifts, grants, and contracts. Since 1974, UW has been the number one public university in America in receiving federal funding for research and training (University of Washington, 2007). To sustain its successful research mission, the UW has developed work–family supports for faculty, staff, and students for more than 30 years, resulting in tenure clock extensions for faculty and childcare for students in the 1970s, childcare for faculty and staff in the 1980s, a part-time tenure track in 1998, and a transitional support program for faculty in 2001.

The family-friendly policies and programs at UW are largely the result of the efforts of student, faculty, and staff groups working with the offices of Work/Life and the Vice Provost for Academic Personnel. These efforts have been so successful that UW has won several family-friendly awards and grants, including a Washington State Child Care Advantage award in 1991 and the Breastfeeding Coalition of Washington State Outstanding Employer Award in 2006. Between 1991 and 2005, UW won more than $1.5 million in competitive state and federal grants for childcare center facility development and expansion (i.e., capital) and tuition subsidy support for students.

In 2001, UW received one of the first National Science Foundation (NSF) ADVANCE Institutional Transformation grants to "advance" the number of women among the faculty and academic leadership of science, engineering, and mathematics departments. The awards were given to institutions that demonstrated that they would be able to achieve institutional change (e.g., institutions that were already moving in a positive direction). Through this ADVANCE grant, UW began a series of leadership development workshops for department chairs as well as institutional research related to flexible policy options for faculty. The leadership development workshops are quarterly half-day events that cover topics such as the basics of budget management, communication skills, and supporting the work–life balance of faculty. The key is selecting department chairs who have experience with the day's topic and having them present to their peers. These workshops are so successful that they have been offered nationally since 2004 and a model for replication has been published (Quinn, Yen, Riskin, & Lange, 2007).

In the spring of 2005, newly appointed UW president Mark Emmert launched the Leadership, Community and Values Initiative (LCVI) in an effort to create community and a common vision of the university's goals and values. This initiative included a climate survey of all faculty and staff that found that many UW employees experience work–life conflict. Data from the 2005 and 2008 LCVI surveys indicate that most UW faculty and staff (89%) are at least somewhat satisfied with the work flexibility they have to accommodate family or personal needs, 85% agree that UW is supportive of faculty and staff who are attempting to balance family and career, and 83% agree that faculty and staff with young children can thrive professionally at UW. UW's leadership recognizes that to compete globally and to attract and retain the best and brightest faculty, staff, and students, more needs to be done to support work–life balance.

Finally, changes in undergraduate education and the shift in the focus of the UW Student Life office toward a commitment to students' whole development—mind, body, purpose, spirit, and meaning—has created new opportunities to grow childcare and emergency support initiatives. As resources have been realigned to support students beyond the classroom, increased services are available including a new student–parent resource center, better access and communication regarding health and wellness offerings (e.g., counseling services, safe-campus programs), and a thoughtful approach to ensuring that students and families in difficult situations are provided a safe transition. These offerings are a fundamental support for helping students balance their work and personal lives.

Whether focused on faculty, staff, or students, efforts to improve the conditions for caregivers at UW show the importance of work–family cultural change. For caregivers to make use of available resources, the environment must support use of family-friendly policies and programs (Drago et al., 2005; Drago, Crouter, Wardell, & Willits, 2001). True cultural change is a slow process that takes not only time, but also a willingness among community members to move beyond their comfort zones, to learn new ways of doing business, and to unlearn outdated notions of both work and family (Eckel, Green, & Hill, 2001; Keup, Walker, Astin, & Lindholm, 2001). With this context in mind, we offer UW's best practices for supporting a diverse campus community and working toward work–family cultural change.

Flexible Work Arrangements

Time has become a scarce resource for staff and faculty. As a result, flexible work arrangements (FWAs) are one of the top indicators of work–life quality and employee satisfaction. The need for FWAs increases as the number of caregivers in the workforce increases. Employees are working longer hours and commuting longer distances, and the global market is driving 24/7 workweeks that conflict with the daily schedules of many families. FWAs cost little to implement, yet they provide a desirable employee benefit (i.e., control over one's schedule). However, developing and implementing FWAs does not necessarily lead to faculty and staff use of the options. Department chairs, managers, and supervisors are crucial to program and policy implementation. Therefore, a necessary component of flexible arrangements is providing managers with the tools, training, and rationale for why FWAs make good business sense.

Work expectations for faculty and staff differ, so flexible work arrangements for each are discussed separately. UW's best practices for FWAs for faculty include tenure clock extension and part-time tenure track. The best practice for UW staff is the range of options available, including flex time, compressed workweeks, telecommuting, and part-time work or job sharing.

Faculty Options

Although there is a great deal of flexibility in when and where faculty can perform their duties, the tenure clock, the pressure on many faculty to bring in external research funding, and the need to juggle research, publication, teaching, and service has increased the time demands on many faculty members (Jacobs & Winslow, 2004). Consequently, faculty need flexible options such as tenure clock extensions and part-time tenure-track appointments. At UW, both of these policies are available.

Tenure Clock Extension

UW faculty have had the option to extend the tenure clock for various personal and professional reasons since the 1970s. Faculty can request that a year in which personal or professional circumstances disrupted the "regular dedication to research" not count toward the probationary period before mandatory tenure review. Likewise, a year in which a faculty member took six months' leave or more does not count as a productive year toward tenure review. Faculty are encouraged to request the extension as soon as possible, but there are no time limits on eligibility.

A 2007 study of a 7-year cohort of assistant professors hired into tenure-track positions at UW indicated that about 25% of faculty used UW's tenure clock extension policy. A higher proportion of women than men used the policy for personal and family reasons, and a higher proportion of men than women used the policy for professional reasons. No difference was found in the rate of tenure attainment between faculty who used the extension and those who did not. A subset of faculty who used the extension were surveyed about their experiences and, although all respondents were granted tenure, 68% agreed that they "would not have made tenure without receiving the tenure clock extension(s)." Most (18 of 19) indicated that using the extension was the "right choice" for them in hindsight. Respondents were asked to provide additional detail about their experience using the tenure clock extension. Feedback included the following: "It provided me with mental security, even though I did not in the end need any extra time" (male, professional field); "I don't believe that I would have achieved tenure without this extension" (male, arts/humanities/social sciences); "I desperately needed that extra year" (female, allied health); and, "Without the stop, I'm not sure I would have wanted to stay in academia" (female, professional field). These responses suggest that the tenure clock extension is a beneficial option for faculty.

Many institutions are beginning to offer tenure clock stops or extensions but seem to be restricting eligibility to women or reasons related to childbirth or adoption. Tips for replicating an inclusive tenure clock extension program like the one at UW include the following:

> *Structure the option so that both men and women are eligible to use it.* This helps alleviate perceptions that the policy is an accommodation for women and make a statement about gender equity.
>
> *Include a range of eligible reasons for an extension (i.e., not just for childbirth or adoption).* Permitting a range of eligible reasons keeps the policy from becoming a "mommy track" or a privilege reserved for parents. Including other forms of intense caregiving, personal medical reasons, and professional reasons such as loss of lab space makes the policy inclusive and helps work toward a more "life-friendly" campus.
>
> *Encourage faculty to request the extension soon after the triggering event, but allow faculty to request it years later.* Some faculty may be afraid of career repercussions if they ask to invoke a flexible policy and may wait until it becomes clear that their tenure review may be in jeopardy if they do not use a flexible policy option.
>
> *Encourage department chairs to discuss extensions at annual reviews.* Regular discussion of policy availability helps faculty see flexible policy use as part of a normal faculty career path and provides frequent opportunities for faculty to request flexible policy options.

Part-Time Tenure Track

In 1998, the UW Faculty Senate passed legislation changing the Faculty Code to permit faculty appointed at half time or more to remain on the tenure track both pre-and post-tenure. The Part-Time Tenure policy prorates the time that a faculty member has from the point of renewal (third-year review) to the mandatory year of tenure review (the sixth year for full-time faculty). Half-time faculty members have 9 years before tenure review.

Since its inception, few faculty have availed themselves of the part-time tenure option and, of those who did, most did so post-tenure or in late career. In 2003, a study that explored the experiences of part-time faculty at UW found some inconsistencies in how the option was implemented at the department level and that part-time faculty were negotiating with their chairs to establish the reduced appointments (Quinn, Lange, Riskin, & Yen, 2004). Establishing expectations for a part-time research agenda was particularly challenging. As one male associate professor put it:

> It is not clear to other people what are the research expectations of me. Should I be doing half as much research because I am spending half of my time at home? Or should I do more research because I actually have more time? Or should I be doing the same amount of research because there is some kind of balancing act there? . . . [I]t is clearly not an easy thing for anyone to look at.

The part-time faculty members in the 2003 study could readily list challenges that part-time faculty members may face, yet each stated that the benefits outweighed the challenges and that they would use the policy again. Within the past few years, the number of pre-tenure faculty using the part-time option has been increasing, particularly among women in science and engineering. Part-time pre-tenure faculty indicate that they appreciate having the extra time available to spend with young children or aging parents without having to give up their academic careers. Late-career part-timers appreciated being able to volunteer and serve on boards (e.g., for the performing arts) before full-time retirement (Quinn, Lange, & Riskin, 2004). All part-time faculty interviewed were adamant about the need to be able to say "no." One male full professor put it most succinctly: "[Other faculty] will take what they can get and so you have to learn to say no . . . if you aren't willing to say no, you will have a hard time with a part-time situation."

Tips for replicating a successful part-time tenure track include the following:

> *Define expectations of part-time faculty in writing and evaluate them using these expectations.* There are challenges in defining the expectations of half-time faculty when the expectations of full-time faculty are often vague. If there are standard teaching loads for full-time faculty, these

can be prorated. Research expectations are typically less well-defined than teaching. Share established expectations with tenure review committee members.

Establish methods to meet departmental teaching requirements when a faculty member shifts to part-time status. Using recaptured salary, find ways to cover the classes previously taught by a newly part-time faculty member without overburdening other department members.

Staff Options

Unlike faculty, many staff positions have traditional or fixed hours during a standard workweek. Flexible work arrangements (FWAs) for staff provide flexibility in when and/or where work is conducted. Experience and research have confirmed that FWAs can have significant organizational benefits, such as increased productivity, lower absenteeism, and reduced turnover (Halpern, 2005). Likewise, staff with access to FWAs tend to have increased job satisfaction and personal satisfaction with their ability to meet their own needs while still contributing to the organization (Halpern, 2005). FWAs are a solid business practice that UW supports when they meet the operational needs of the unit and the employee.

UW is composed of diverse work environments that include two medical centers and a large institution that operates 24 hours a day, 7 days a week. Staffing needs are complex and require a range of management tools. Implementation of FWAs must be at the unit or department level and must include consideration of established policies and labor contracts that impact work schedules. Increasing the complexity, not all staff positions are conducive to flexibility in where work is done. An example is an office receptionist who has direct, in-person contact with clients (i.e., the work must be done at the reception desk). However, there could be flexibility in when the work is done if two staff members share the responsibility to cover the reception desk hours. With these constraints in mind, the best practices at UW for FWAs for staff include flex time, compressed workweeks, telecommuting, and part-time work or job sharing.

Flex Time

Flex-time work arrangements have a range of starting and ending times for the workday with a mandatory "core" time in the middle of the day, increasing flexibility in when staff work. Using the example of two receptionists responsible for staffing a front desk between 8 a.m. and 5 p.m., one may prefer to work 7:00 a.m. to 3:30 p.m. with a half-hour lunch and the other 9 a.m. to 6 p.m. with an hour-long lunch. When both are allowed to use flex time, the front desk could be staffed from 7 a.m. to 6 p.m., extending overall service provision while enabling each staff member to schedule work time in a way that may facilitate completion of personal tasks.

Compressed Workweeks

A schedule in which staff work 40 hours in fewer than 5 days, such as four 10-hour days a week or 9 days out of 10 in a 2-week schedule, is considered a compressed workweek. Staff frequently request that their compressed workweek include a consistent day off. Mondays and Fridays are common; however, a midweek day off can also provide much needed work–life balance. These options increase flexibility in when work is done.

Telecommuting

Increasing flexibility in where work is done, telecommuting allows staff to use telecommunications and computer technology to regularly work from home or an alternative work site. A telecommuting arrangement may be mutually established between a supervisor and an employee, or may be required because of the nature of the position. UW recognizes telecommuting as an option that can meet a variety of interests and enhance employee satisfaction and productivity, reduce commute trips, and address space restrictions.

Part-Time Work or Job Sharing

Part-time work is a regular arrangement consisting of a workweek that is less than the standard 40 hours per week. Part-time work can attract and retain trained and experienced staff who are not able or willing to work full time because of personal commitments. It is a viable strategy that provides people with time to balance work and home life. Job sharing often comprises one full-time position that is equally shared between two employees with pro-rated salary, benefits, and paid time off. Both employees are equally responsible for the success of the position.

A 2003 UW survey of employees in the Service Employees International Union (SEIU) Local 925 bargaining unit revealed that 80% of those who requested FWAs received them. One respondent stated, "I am working part time on a relatively regular schedule that integrates my personal needs as well as the needs of my office. Although my schedule is generally static, I have the flexibility to change my schedule around as life circumstance presents itself and all with the support of my manager. It is wonderful!"

Tips for implementing flexible work arrangements for staff include the following:

> *Perform workforce planning of the entire work team, evaluating the appropriateness of flexible work arrangements for each position.* Not all positions/people will be conducive to flexible work arrangements. Keep in mind the business needs of the unit; could service provision be extended by having staggered, overlapping shifts? Does the individual's work style and history support the demands of the arrangement?
>
> *Include the work team in the planning process.* This helps members of the unit take ownership of the process and creates buy-in. Inclusion also ensures that all parties are aware of the details and potential impact of the FWAs.
>
> *Always pilot new initiatives.* University leaders are usually willing to try a new program for a fixed period, rather than adopting new programs. Usage data from a pilot can help make policy improvements or demonstrate the need for policy institutionalization. All participants must be prepared to return to preflexibility arrangements if the situation requires.
>
> *Document details of the arrangements.* Flexible work arrangements can initially be somewhat complicated to administer, so it is especially important that such arrangements be well documented and understood by the employee, manager, and co-workers.

Childcare

For many of UW's parents of young children, access to affordable, quality childcare is fundamental to being able to participate in work or school. Similarly, reliable childcare helps faculty, staff, and students remain productive on campus. UW has acknowledged the importance of childcare for several decades and has developed a multifaceted program that addresses parental choice. However, like many campuses, UW is facing a demand for childcare that is far greater than the capacity of its on-site childcare facilities. Compounding the problem, Seattle, like many areas throughout the country, is facing a shortage of affordable, quality childcare, which increases the burden on UW to accommodate the children of its community members. Recent challenges in recruiting "star" faculty members have made childcare a visible element of recruitment and retention. This is particularly true for female faculty in academic fields that were traditionally dominated by men, such as science, engineering, and math. In these areas, UW competes with other leading academic institutions and industry for talented women, which significantly increases the challenge of recruiting and retaining female faculty. Consequently, increasing the childcare available to faculty, staff, and students has become a critical issue for the University of Washington.

Fortunately, many of UW's academic leaders understand the importance of childcare. Buy-in from academic leaders is key and provides a vital leverage point. As an example, a new UW dean almost lost a highly desired faculty recruit over the lack of available childcare, leading him to become a powerful and vocal advocate for increasing available childcare slots for faculty. Such situations help make the argument that childcare is a valuable recruitment tool and not merely another benefit. Even with this understanding, the discussion always comes down to resources. There are competing demands for limited resources, and childcare frequently competes with salary, tuition remission, and various other important issues. However, it is heartening that the issue of childcare is on the table with these other important issues and is being actively explored.

To better understand the issue and importance of childcare at UW, the provost established a campuswide Child Care Advisory Committee in the fall of 2006 to review short- and long-term childcare options and provide recommendations for future action. The group confirmed that long wait lists for the campus childcare centers, limited availability of infant and toddler care in the community, and the high cost of care were creating gaps in the university's ability to meet the increasing demand from students, staff, and faculty for childcare. It identified three primary issues: (1) access, (2) affordability, and (3) quality of childcare.

Existing Programs

Childcare supports have been in place at UW for several decades. In the early 1970s, UW established the Childcare Assistance Program for Students (also known as the Childcare Voucher Program). The program provides financial assistance to eligible students (based on income) to subsidize childcare services. The program has been funded by a portion of the Services and Activities Fee that all UW students pay. In the late 1980s, a staff position was created to focus exclusively on the childcare needs of faculty and staff. This period marked the beginning of the availability of sick childcare, monthly parent education, and collaboration with community-based childcare centers for priority access to UW families. All of these steps helped create a program of childcare resources that is low-cost to the university and provides parents with multiple options. UW's best practices on childcare include on-site childcare facilities, resource and referral services, financial assistance for students, and an online Caregiver Directory.

On-Site Childcare Facilities

UW provides 259 on-site childcare spaces for infants, toddlers, and preschoolers in six campus facilities. Faculty and staff have priority for slots in three of the facilities, and students have priority in the other three. The capital projects that created this capacity were funded through a variety of sources and collaborations including student family housing, state grants (e.g., State Department Social and Health Services grants, Washington State Higher Education Coordinating Board grants), central administrative funding, and student activities fees. Although both space and funding are typically scarce resources, we have found that whenever there is funding, space can be found.

Resource and Referral Services

Through a contract with a local childcare resource and referral agency for enhanced service, UW faculty, staff, and students have 24/7 access to an online resource, phone support from a childcare specialist, vacancy searches of licensed childcare in the area, and other services. This childcare support saves families a tremendous amount of time searching for childcare vacancies. The agency also works to expand the availability of community-based childcare as well as to enhance the quality of care, thus addressing the issue of accessibility to affordable, quality childcare.

Financial Assistance for Students

Funded through the student Services and Activities Fee, the student childcare assistance program is a long-standing program that provides both access and parental choice to student parents. Based on income eligibility, students receive vouchers equal to up to 60% of their childcare expenses that can be used at any licensed childcare center. This portable voucher serves both graduate and undergraduate students. Between 2001 and 2005, this program had an additional $500,000 in funding from a federal Department of Education Child Care Access Means Parents in School (CCAMPIS) grant.

Online Posting System

Also referred to as the Caregiver Directory, this Web-based directory provides a venue for both caregivers and employers to post their needs within the UW community. Caregivers are those seeking employment to earn money caring for children, elders, or adult dependents; running errands; or doing light housekeeping. They may make themselves available for full-time, part-time, short-term, or intermittent work.

Even with these resources and services, serious gaps exist regarding accessibility, affordability, and quality. Without additional resources, these gaps will continue to grow. The university has begun to address some of these issues. The 2008 budget adopted by the board of regents included new funding to enhance the childcare resource and referral service and to purchase priority access to a block of childcare spaces in the community. These spaces allow the university to provide immediate access for recruitment or retention of a limited number of high-level faculty and staff. Long-term plans are being developed that will create a comprehensive approach to addressing campuswide needs. As the Seattle housing market continues to rise beyond the reach of most junior faculty and staff, UW is exploring options to develop affordable housing that would include on-site childcare. Additionally, the institution is discussing the development of a new lab school to increase available childcare and teacher training for students in early childhood development programs in UW's College of Education. By taking a broad view of the needs and looking for a comprehensive solution to multiple issues, UW can leverage challenging problems by addressing them together, rather than as individual, separate issues that are competing for limited resources.

Strategies for Childcare Expansion

Campuses need to be alert for and responsive to various opportunities to increase the availability of childcare for the campus community. At the University of Washington, the following key strategies have been effective:

Develop grant-seeking behaviors. Regularly scan the landscape for outside funding sources such as federal, state, and private foundations. The federal Department of Education and state human services agencies have allocated funding for early childhood initiatives. Private foundations that support early childhood development will consider funding daycare facilities and/or playground enhancement.

Collaborate with academic and service units. Work with other colleges and departments on campus to find ways to access research dollars or intern sites for students in academic programs with a practicum component related to early childhood development. Housing expansion projects for students and faculty can include childcare and family-friendly rooms (e.g., lactation stations, changing rooms, and child/family-friendly spaces). Creative partnerships can achieve a common goal that meets differing needs.

Emergency Support

UW has developed supports for faculty, staff, and students experiencing various unexpected life events or emergencies. These supports help individuals get through temporary transitions or life events that may be potentially career threatening for faculty or staff or may lead to student dropout or stop-out (temporary leave from the university). Helping employees through periods of crisis greatly increases the likelihood that they will remain with the university. Investing in employees during these periods ensures that they will return to their normal levels of productivity and engagement. Successful emergency supports reflect the differing needs of faculty, staff, and students. At UW, a best practice for providing emergency support for faculty is the Transitional Support Program. The showcased staff option is shared leave.

Transitional Support Program for Faculty

For many faculty, temporary reductions in productivity can result in a stalled research program or a derailed academic career. Rather than permitting a temporary circumstance to undermine the career of a UW faculty member, the Transitional Support Program (TSP) was developed in 2001 through the UW ADVANCE Center for Institutional Change, funded by the National Science Foundation (NSF), and was available to faculty within the 21 departments participating in the ADVANCE program at UW. In June 2004, UW's

Office of the Provost extended the TSP to all faculty. The TSP offers financial support to help outstanding faculty members maintain their productivity while experiencing potentially career-threatening crises such as severe personal illness, severe or acute family illness, childbirth complications, or other critical situations. The funding typically covers release from teaching and/or research support to help faculty members keep up their research programs during times of crisis. For a relatively small amount of money, the huge costs of replacing a faculty member or losing a research program can be avoided.

The program is evidence of the university's commitment to helping faculty balance work and life and has been extremely valuable for faculty productivity and morale. Many TSP recipients noted that when they received TSP assistance, it was the first time in their faculty careers that they felt as if an institution was invested in their success. For example, both members of an academic couple that experienced a family crisis received a TSP grant. They made it through the crisis with their research programs intact, and one has since been successfully reviewed for tenure. Competitive offers have been made to both faculty, and they have refused them. The couple indicated that the support they received from the university during their time of family crisis is a major factor in their desire to stay. Successes such as this have made UW's TSP a model for other colleges and universities seeking ways to support faculty during difficult transitions (Riskin, Lange, Quinn, Yen, & Brainard, 2007). One of our ongoing challenges is to market the program to chairs to ensure that faculty who need the program have access to it.

Tips for replicating a successful transitional support program for faculty include the following:

> *Structure the program as an award for meritorious faculty rather than an accommodation.* This will help avoid any stigmatization of receiving the award. Likewise, use (reasonably) broad terms in the program description to encourage a wide variety of proposals, rather than listing all anticipated life transitions. This will increase the inclusiveness of the program. To increase the responsiveness of the program and reduce potential abuses, specify that awards can be reassessed if circumstances change and the transitional support is no longer needed.
> *Include key stakeholders such as chairs and deans in program planning and development* so that they buy into the program and market it to their

faculty. Faculty need to see that their chairs and deans support use of new programs before they will be confident using them.

Shared Paid Leave for Staff

The shared-leave program allows Washington state employees to donate part of their accrued annual leave, sick leave, and/or personal holiday hours to co-workers whose own accrued leave has been depleted and who will need to take leave without pay or separate from employment because of extraordinary circumstances. All regular state employees who accrue leave and who meet eligibility requirements may donate and receive shared leave. An employee is eligible to receive shared leave for a severe, extraordinary, or life-threatening illness or injury, or if he or she has caregiver responsibilities for a relative or a household member with a severe, extraordinary, or life-threatening illness or injury, and the employee has used or is about to use all of his or her eligible annual and sick leave. Shared leave enhances the feeling of community and the culture of supporting one's colleagues. The approach to replicate shared leave at other colleges and universities will depend on their status as public or private institutions. To our colleagues in the public sector, this concept was embraced by the legislature and also supported by labor unions. It provides a meaningful way for colleagues to support each other in a time of need and has the additional benefit of building community.

Tips for replicating a shared-leave program for staff include the following:

> *Review shared-leave policies at the state and local level as well as at peer institutions.* Many universities can base their shared-leave policies on locally relevant rules and policies or on the policies of similar colleges or universities. Peer benchmarking studies can also provide necessary data and evidence to encourage campus policy makers to adopt shared-leave and other policies that are prevalent at competing institutions.
>
> *Promote the importance of community and of supporting colleagues in need.* A shared-leave policy, though critically important to those in need, also provides a tangible venue for building community. Donating or receiving leave helps build employee commitment to the university community and helps shift the workplace culture from an individualistic-competition model to one of teamwork and collaboration.

Conclusion

No single initiative or effort brought about work–family cultural change at the University of Washington. Developing an inclusive family-friendly environment in a large, decentralized university requires collaboration with many campus stakeholders. The success of cultural change efforts depends on nurturing existing alliances and building new partnerships with any group that shares an interest in the issue or the potential outcome. The key is to be able both to recognize and respond to opportunities as they arise, and to initiate change efforts when the time is right. This strategy permitted UW to win an Alfred P. Sloan Award for Faculty Career Flexibility and create Balance@UW.

We are proud of our accomplishments to date, but fully appreciate that there is still room for significant improvement. Responses to the 2008 LCVI survey indicate that 39% of faculty were impacted by the lack of childcare during the previous 12 months, compared to 17% of staff. Similarly, 25% of faculty and 21% of staff were impacted by elder care. Using these data points as key indicators will help support efforts to keep moving the University of Washington forward along the family-friendly continuum. True cultural change takes time (Eckel, Hill, Green, & Mallon, 1999), and a crucial element in these change efforts is having the patience to stay the course. National trends clearly indicate that work–family flexibility is on the horizon for higher education. This change is coming and, as this book demonstrates, many models of best practices exist for the next waves of institutions to follow.

References

American Council on Education. (2005). *An agenda for excellence: Creating flexibility in tenure-track faculty careers.* Washington, DC: Author.

Bickel, J., & Brown, A. J. (2005). Generation X: Implications for faculty recruitment and development in academic health centers. *Academic Medicine, 80*(3), 205–210.

Blackburn, R. T., & Hollenshead, C. (1999). *University of Michigan faculty work-life study report.* Ann Arbor: Center for the Study of Higher and Postsecondary Education, University of Michigan.

Committee on Maximizing the Potential of Women in Academic Science and Engineering. (2006). *Beyond bias and barriers: Fulfilling the potential of women in academic science and engineering.* Washington, DC: National Academies Press.

Drago, R., & Colbeck, C. (2003). *The mapping project: Exploring the terrain of U.S. colleges and universities for faculty and families*. University Park: Pennsylvania State University.

Drago, R., Colbeck, C., Stauffer, K. D., Pirretti, A., Burkum, K., Fazioli, J., et al. (2005). Bias against caregiving. *Academe, 91*(5), 22–25.

Drago, R., Crouter, A. C., Wardell, M., & Willits, B. S. (2001). *Final report of the faculty and families project*. University Park: Pennsylvania State University.

Eckel, P., Green, M. F., & Hill, B. (2001). *On change. Riding the waves of change: Insights from transforming institutions*. Washington, DC: American Council on Education.

Eckel, P., Hill, B., Green, M., & Mallon, B. (1999). *On change. Reports from the road: Insights on institutional change*. Washington, DC: American Council on Education.

Friedman, D. E., Rimsky, C., & Johnson, A. A. (1996). *College and university reference guide to work-family programs: Report on a collaborative study*. New York: Families & Work Institute.

Gappa, J. M., & MacDermid, S. M. (1997). *Work, family, and the faculty career. New pathways: Faculty career and employment for the 21st century working paper series, inquiry #8*. Washington, DC: Association of American Higher Education.

Halpern, D. F. (2005). How time-flexible work policies can reduce stress, improve health, and save money. *Stress and Health, 23*(3), 157–168.

Hensel, N. (1991). *Realizing gender equality in higher education: The need to integrate work/family issues*. ASHE-ERIC Higher Education Report No. 2. Washington, DC: George Washington University, School of Education and Human Development.

Jacobs, J. A., & Winslow, S. E. (2004). Overworked faculty: Job stresses and family demands. *Annals of the AAPSS, 596*, 104–129.

Keup, J. R., Walker, A. A., Astin, H. S., & Lindholm, J. A. (2001). *Organizational culture and institutional transformation:* ERIC Clearinghouse on Higher Education, Washington, DC. ED464521.

Lancaster, L. C., & Stillman, D. (2003). *When generations collide: Who they are, why they clash, how to solve the generational puzzle at work*. New York: HarperBusiness.

Mason, M. A., & Goulden, M. (2002). Do babies matter? The effect of family formation on the lifelong careers of academic men and women. *Academe, 88*(6), 21–27.

Massachusetts Institute of Technology (MIT). (1999). *A study on the status of women faculty in science at MIT*. Cambridge, MA: Author.

Quinn, K., Lange, S. E., & Riskin, E. A. (2004). *Part-time tenure track policies: Assessing utilization*. Paper presented at the Women in Engineering Programs and Advocates Network, Albuquerque, NM.

Quinn, K., Lange, S. E., Riskin, E. A., & Yen, J. (2004). *Exploring part-time tenure track policy at the University of Washington: Final report to the Alfred P. Sloan Foundation.* Seattle: University of Washington.

Quinn, K., Yen, J., Riskin, E. A., & Lange, S. E. (2007). Leadership development workshops for department chairs: A model for enabling family-friendly cultural change. *Change, 39*(4), 42–47.

Raabe, P. (1997). Work-family policies for faculty: How "career-and family-friendly" is academe? In M. A. Ferber & J. W. Loeb (Eds.), *Academic couples: Problems and promises* (pp. 208–225). Urbana: University of Illinois Press.

Riskin, E. A., Lange, S. E., Quinn, K., Yen, J., & Brainard, S. G. (2007). Supporting faculty during life transitions. In A. J. Stewart, J. E. Malley, & D. Lavaque-Manty (Eds.), *Transforming science and engineering: Advancing academic women* (pp. 116–130). Ann Arbor: University of Michigan Press.

University of Washington. (2007). UW profile. Retrieved March 21, 2008, from http://www.washington.edu/newsroom/profile/research.html

Wolf-Wendel, L., & Ward, K. (2006). Faculty work and family life: Policy perspectives from different institutional types. In S. J. Bracken, J. K. Allen, & D. R. Dean (Eds.), *The balancing act: Gendered perspectives in faculty roles and work lives* (pp. 51–72). Sterling, VA: Stylus.

3

CONNECTING WORK AND LIFE AT THE UNIVERSITY OF ARIZONA

Strategic Practice by UA Life & Work Connections

Caryn S. Jung, David L. Swihart, and Darci A. Thompson

You can't run a business without people. Only people can serve. Only people can lead, only people can innovate and create. Putting people first leads to organizational success.

—William Pollard, *Soul of a Firm*

Literature consistently uses terms such as "work/life" and "work/family" to describe evolving work and life experiences for employees, and how such experiences impact workplace effectiveness (Grzywacz & Carlson, 2007; Sloan Work & Family Research Network, n.d., 2006; Wayne, Grzywacz, Carlson, & Kacmar, 2007). Aware of this, many employers offer work–life assistance to their employees to try to improve workplace effectiveness and to aid recruitment and retention efforts. UA Life & Work Connections (LWC) is the University of Arizona's designated work–life unit for faculty and staff. The program was developed over time by integrating work–life services, employee assistance, and worksite wellness. This chapter outlines this process, focusing on several key points: (a) the seamless integration of professional life-cycle programs informed by a social ecology of health model, (b) the hybrid design that allows for timely responses throughout the campus environment, and (c) the transferability of this research-based practice model to other settings.

In many ways, workforce trends at UA have been similar to the national experiences of peer institutions during the 1980s and 1990s. For example, the increased numbers of female faculty and staff (often in dual-income families) who expressed a need for childcare assistance. These needs gave rise to family-friendly workplace changes at UA. Conversations focused on the following issues: (a) centrally located services, (b) providing resource, referral, and professional advisement, (c) financing childcare costs, and (d) designating an office to manage family inquiries and oversee future projects. Support for the initiative was generated by a campuswide study that revealed that employees have great difficulty maintaining balanced lives. This finding was in contrast to an earlier faculty survey taken when most respondents were men over age 50 (Kolodny, 1998).

The research outcomes suggested several points. First, the university should review and broaden its definition of *family*. Second, a childcare coordinator position should be established and an office expanded to "embrace a larger definition of multigenerational family care requirement . . . as . . . the numbers of those over sixty-five increase, eldercare services may be even more in demand than childcare" (Kolodny, 1998, p. 291). The University of Arizona was responsive to these events. The campus childcare office was created and within a year was housed within LWC, with a program coordinator responsible for its operation.

The early development of LWC, however, began in the area of wellness. Although it is now linked with social ecology of health, LWC was originally independent of a directly applied social ecology of health model. Once fully developed, the specific articulation of LWC's practice model (Thompson & Swihart, 2005) bore such strong philosophical ties to social ecology that the latter has become a guiding standard for the former. For this reason, an overview of the social ecology of health provides context, followed by a description of LWC's program.

Social Ecology of Health

Social ecology is a theory of human development that pertains to the relationships and transactions between human beings and their environment, with emphasis on social, institutional, and cultural contexts (e.g., Stokols,

Pelletier, & Fielding, 1996). In the preface to his foundational book on the subject, Urie Bronfenbrenner (1979) stated unequivocally how the interactive process between the person and his or her environment influences human development:

> Whether parents can perform effectively in their own child-rearing roles within the family depends on role demands, stresses and supports emanating from other settings . . . parents' evaluation of their own capacity to function, as well as their view of their child, are related to such external factors as flexibility of job schedules, adequacy of child care arrangements . . . the presence of friends . . . the quality of health and social services . . . availability of supportive settings is . . . a function of their existence and frequency in a given culture or subculture. (p. 7)

Social ecology posits that the individual is a part of, and interacts with, his or her immediate environment (*microsystems,* such as home or workgroup). When multiple microsystems are considered together, they form a *mesosystem.* These layers are nested within a larger system called an *exosystem* (e.g., a department or institution), which, in turn, is also nested within the broader cultural system, or *macrosystem* (Bronfenbrenner, 1979; Bronfenbrenner & Ceci, 1994; Grzywacz & Fuqua, 2000). When change occurs in one part of a system, it forces a corresponding change in the other systems. These nested systems are mechanisms through which forces of scale are transmitted up and down, back and forth. Within this context of shifting changes, human development occurs through *ecological transitions* (Bronfenbrenner, 1979; Bronfenbrenner & Ceci, 1994), which are major life cycle changes (e.g., adulthood, midlife transition) and minor ones (e.g., learning to more skillfully manage relationships). There are also *work-cycle* changes that are developmental transitions (e.g., becoming a supervisor).

Implementing change beyond superficial influences thus involves both the individual and one or more environmental systems. A potentially useful corollary is that programs to intervene or assist employees are likely to be more effective when applied to the predominant mesosystem (e.g., work and family), by viewing these settings as "leverage points" (Bronfenbrenner & Ceci, 1994; Grzywacz & Fuqua, 2000; Stokols, 1996; Stokols et al., 1996). As a result, LWC services are deliberately designed to influence the institution at a number of levels, including committee involvement, workplace violence prevention, and individualized services.

Researchers (Frone, Russell, & Cooper, 1997; Grzywacz, 2000; Stokols, 1996) have taken Bronfenbrenner's hypotheses and studied their application to the field of health. The findings demonstrate the difficulty in distinguishing independent causation of stress effects variously on physical health, work–family health, and mental health. Note that these domains correspond to effects that, in the workplace, are addressed by wellness, work–life, and employee assistance programs. This suggests that interventions and services from a whole-person, integrated source hold potential for a higher level of effectiveness (Frone et al., 1997; Grzywacz, 2000; Grzywacz, Almeida, & McDonald, 2002; Grzywacz & Fuqua, 2000; Grzywacz & Marks, 2000a, 2000b; Hammer, Cullen, Neal, Sinclair, & Shafiro, 2005; Stokols, 1996; Stokols et al., 1996).

Some other remarkable findings have surfaced as well, including the fact that the ways that stress from home affects people at work are different from the ways work stress affects people at home. Dysfunctional ways of coping in the two situations are different. Grzywacz and his colleagues (Grzywacz, 2000; Grzywacz et al., 2002; Grzywacz & Marks, 2000a, 2000b) operationalized these influences as *negative spillover* and directionalized it as from either work to family (w → f) or family to work (f → w). Conversely, *positive spillover,* also bidirectional, refers to where the influence is harmonizing and not conflictual. They have solidly demonstrated that the four permutations of spillover (positive w → f, positive f → w, negative w → f, negative f → w) are nearly independent of one another (*orthogonal*), result in distinctive behavioral outcomes depending on direction, have cumulative effects (opposites do not cancel), and are not equally powerful (Frone et al., 1997; Grzywacz, 2000; Grzywacz et al., 2002; Grzywacz & Bass, 2003; Grzywacz & Marks, 2000a, 2000b; Hammer et al., 2005). If these findings are valid in higher education settings, they hold unusual potential for guiding the allocation of scarce family-friendly resources in ways that could target needs, reduce specific deleterious effects, and lead to high return on investment (Grzywacz, 2000).

Consider a tenure-track assistant professor who is 1 year away from submitting her dossier for tenure, but falls behind in publishing because her newborn must be fed several times a night. Here, the dual forces of work performance pressure and motherhood collide and create spillover. The two microsystems of work and family are in conflict and have resulted in degraded work performance because of sleep deprivation. Other results may include stress, a deteriorating relationship with her partner and child, and a major threat to her career. Note that these circumstances do not necessarily impact her friendships or finances, but they do exert significant influence at work and at home, thus confirming these settings as leverage points.

What would an appropriate response be from a social ecology of health (SEH)-based integrated program? The specific details vary from one person to the next, but the broad answer is generally consistent: Offer as many options and services as possible while sensitively helping the person see her options and choices from a developmental perspective.

This is the most pivotal concept of SEH, that it is a model of human development. In this example, the dilemma forces the professor to consider strategies and resources from which she can select. Many combinations of possible services exist, such as lactation resources, flex time, couples counseling, family medical leave, infant nutrition information, temporarily stopping the tenure clock, and dependent-care information. But as she chooses out of developmental awareness, she becomes increasingly effective in her chosen environment, based on her values, goals, and priorities, over and above mere problem solving. This concept makes SEH a powerful basis for family-friendly programs such as work–life, employee assistance, and wellness programs. It empowers individuals and promotes intrinsic motivation and self-efficacy. These qualities are at the core of resiliency.

These developmental concepts of social ecology of health, including whole-person needs, life-cycle issues, and spillover, provide context for understanding the development and functioning of UA Life & Work Connections.

The University of Arizona

Established in 1885 as the first university in the Arizona Territory and the state's only land-grant institution, the University of Arizona in Tucson embraces its threefold mission of excellence in teaching, research, and public service. An RU/VH (research university, very high activity) institution and member of the Association of American Universities including a large health sciences campus and teaching hospital, UA has approximately 37,000 students and more than 14,600 employees.

As with most universities, UA has a well-established student health center that includes a strong focus on health promotion and prevention. In the late 1980s, forward-thinking leaders in student health noted that no similar programs were available for faculty and staff. As a result, they met with the university's human resources and risk management and safety departments to address this absence. These departments then collaborated to bring Employee Wellness into existence under the aegis of Campus Health. In 1998, the name was changed to Life & Work Connections (LWC) to reflect its broad range of "whole-person" services.

It is not common for a work-life program to be linked with a wellness program, much less grow out of one. The fact that LWC developed this way both comes from and leads to conceptualizing employee needs as interconnected among career, familial, physical, and other domains of human existence. As a result, LWC's mission is unusual:

> In partnership with the State of Arizona, UA Life & Work Connections is dedicated to increasing resiliency, and to increasing workplace productivity and effectiveness in employees and the organization. We do this by identifying, designing and providing specialized services that address the evolving work/life needs of our clients in order to enhance their contribution to the UA and the community.

The basis for this mission statement comes from the belief that resilient people and organizations are more resistant to degradation due to stress in all areas of life; have better adaptive capacities to maintain healthy behaviors and draw on existing resources; and have more confidence in their abilities to problem-solve and find positive outcomes (Norris, Stevens, Pfefferbaum, Wyche, & Pfefferbaum, 2008; Sapolsky, 1999; Siebert, 1996; Thomas, 2000). Integrated, systemic services are important, especially in higher education where the employee population is largely viewed as a "knowledge society," with a premium placed on innovation and creativity (Burud & Tumolo, 2004).

From its inception, faculty and staff responded positively to the new LWC program services. They also revealed more diverse and complex needs reflecting a "whole-person" spectrum, that is, needs that overlap the physical, emotional, intellectual, and psychological domains. Common types of employee concerns included family relationships, family care, conflict with peers and superiors, depression, career progression, and poor health. Almost immediately there was a demand for expanded services.

The timeline for integrating components began with Employee Assistance Counseling/Consultation (EACC), which was added in 1991. Child Care and Family Resources was added in 1995, Elder Care and Life Cycle Resources in 1998, and Work/Life Support in 2001. Professional staff at that point included a doctorate-level registered dietitian, two master's-level, licensed behavioral health professionals, and a master's-level gerontologist with prior corporate work–family experience.

Uniting the five LWC components facilitated strategic and tactical planning in order to provide services using an integrated, whole-person approach. The model developed was later published (see Thompson & Swihart, 2005) amid the growing realization that it fit a social ecology approach. In contrast with institutions that provide "employee-only" or "student-only" services, three of the five LWC programs are offered to students as well as employees. In summary, LWC has five distinct, yet related offerings:

1. *Child Care and Family Resources* offers customized childcare referrals, resources and consultations, financial assistance for qualifying costs in Arizona, a subsidized Sick Child and Emergency/Back-Up Care Program, and educational presentations on childcare and parenting issues.

2. *Elder Care and Life Cycle Resources* offers personalized consultations to assist those caring for dependent older adults, referrals to campus and community resources, and educational presentations on caregiving and aging issues.

3. *Employee Assistance Counseling/Consultation* offers confidential consultations and assessment on a variety of personal and work situations, supervisory consultation, short-term counseling, referrals to community resources, and critical-incident stress management services.

4. *Work/Life Support* provides consultations for alternative work arrangements, a Mommy Connections program lactation subsidy, related lactation resources, and educational presentations.

5. *Worksite Wellness* currently offers heart health screenings, individual nutrition and fitness coaching, elastic bands strength classes, flu vaccinations, planned walking options, educational presentations, and the WellBeing newsletter, a monthly publication distributed to all faculty and staff.

None of LWC's services are contracted out to a third party by the university. The settings for services are deliberately varied across diverse locations: the LWC offices, departmental visits, central or off-site campus locations, and online. As institutional employees, LWC staff are active in campus networks and committees to create a positive influence on both organizational and policy levels.

Integration as a Strategic Approach

The integration of employee assistance, wellness, and work–life programs within the workplace has risen in prominence over the past 20 years. (For an overview on the subject, see Attridge, Herlihy, & Maiden, 2005.) The predominant rationale has reflected the business bottom line: cost savings to the organization in terms of health care expenditures, reductions in absenteeism and presenteeism, and increased productivity (e.g., Attridge, 2005). However, as Roman (2005) and Herlihy (2005) point out, unresolved questions remain. Foremost is an operational definition of integration; second is a description of how it works in actual practice.

Are programs considered integrated when they are simply housed together administratively, or, at the other extreme, when programs are so blended that there are no lines of demarcation between areas such as work–life, wellness, and employee assistance? Roman's (2005) concern for the latter is that integration will bring a loss of identity to employee assistance and, therefore, will water down its distinctive services. Although both Herlihy and Roman raise valid questions, no consensus has been reached regarding a universal description. An operational definition of integration is important for research evaluation because it defines measurable variables. A lack of clarity about how integration works in practice has created problems by referencing a term that has no agreed-on definition or methodology. The management approach taken by the service provider will define the methodology and will also influence whether integration is effective.

LWC defines integration as "bringing together in a synergistic way, the specialized knowledge and trained expertise of professionals in different but related fields, in order to better serve the organization and its employees" (Swihart & Thompson, 2002). The core idea is that professionals in employee assistance, wellness, and dependent care (among others) all contribute collective knowledge, education, and experience to a service and its application. In creative collaboration, colleagues strive to promote a greater, positive impact than would be the case if each worked independently of the others. This definition does not address the form and appearance of services, as flexibility and innovation may influence the creation of a "best fit" service.

Hybrid Design and Timely Responses

A hybrid design is one that includes multifaceted programs that are joined together. Hybrid-designed services uniquely result from seamless integration. They may be informal or formal collaborations and either permanent or temporary as determined by the situation. This flexibility enables swift mobilization of resources for timely responses. One of the most common is a joint presentation, such as LWC's Building Resiliency to Stress. This frequently requested offering brings Employee Assistance Counseling/Consultation and Worksite Wellness together to describe the psychological, emotional, and physiological aspects of stress and offers strategies in these domains to cope and create resistance to stress. Balancing the Spheres of Work and Life is another educational presentation jointly conducted by Work/Life Support and Employee Assistance Counseling/Consultation. The focus here is to address faculty and staff stress as it relates to work–life issues through coping and resiliency-building skills as well as problem-solving strategies.

Whatever the uniquenesses of a family situation, hybrid resources can be quickly mobilized. For example, a faculty member in the "sandwich generation," that is, caring for two children and aging parents simultaneously, came to EACC seeking ways to cope with the stress of living with parents-in-law and tight finances. Both families living under one roof was leading to enmeshment and blurring of family boundaries. To add to the problem, the in-laws were both displaying increasing dementia. They were behaving irrationally, his preschool children did not understand and were distressed, and his wife was showing signs of depression. The faculty member was introduced face-to-face to the elder care professional, who assessed the family's elder care needs. In counseling, the faculty member was also able to determine what to do about his in-laws. According to his feedback, the timeliness of the joint assistance and follow-up visits provided to the professor lifted his burden enormously.

Another hybrid service developed for expedient assistance is LWC's Sick Child and Emergency/Back-Up Care Program (SCP/EBCP). Offered for more than two decades, SCP/EBCP is an effective recruitment and retention tool and has been identified as a factor even with the promise of increased compensation elsewhere. This nationally known program uses contracted vendors that dispatch caregivers to a student's or employee's home to care for a sick child, age birth to 12 years, if he or she is unable to attend school or childcare. This service is also available for emergency backup care when primary childcare suddenly becomes unavailable. The following example describes what happens when an unscheduled interruption in regular care or school arrangements occurs and an immediate resource is needed:

A staff couple's regular childcare provider became ill, and although they had supportive departments and the work–life flexibility to take turns staying home, a series of unusual circumstances made those options impossible that day. After initiating a 5:00 a.m. emergency care request, one parent enthusiastically stated, "It was fantastic! This lady rang our doorbell at 6:00 a.m. with her arms full of paper, crayons, and pencils. When my wife and I returned at 4:00 p.m., our excited daughter couldn't wait to show us all the things she had created!"

Hybrid services can include time-sensitive collaboration with other departments, as in the following example. A single student parent of a young child needed childcare assistance during a personal health crisis. Her need quickly grew beyond an individual inquiry and required a team response. Timing complications included pending finals, the institution's seasonal break and campus closure, and arranging care around an anticipated treatment timeline for the student parent. The ensuing collaboration included faculty, administrators, and LWC and medical personnel and created a foundation for well-planned support and guidance when classes resumed. The integrated and hybrid model can facilitate trust, confidence, and acceptance by students, faculty, staff, and administrators.

Research findings, societal trends, and specific needs continue to drive creative, hybrid services. Part of these are unique to the University of Arizona, whereas others are more general. Many of the underlying concepts and direct services can be adapted to a variety of other settings.

Transferability of the Practice Model: Advantages and Concerns

In our experience, the social ecology of health model provides a number of benefits in terms of successfully responding to the needs of faculty, staff, and students. However, despite its successes, some challenges in implementation remain. We discuss each here.

Advantages

The social ecology of health model offers a way of relating to employees and organizations that applies in many settings. The value of a model is its transferability, and so other organizations can easily incorporate concepts such as home and work leverage points, systemic linkages, life cycle, and spillover into their conceptualization of the organizational needs. The SEH model allows for cultural peculiarities in a specific setting.

LWC's idea of integration is also transferable. A critical requirement is to define how integration and collaboration will work at the practice level and then to adopt those tenets as a mind-set. The advantage here is *integrated assessment,* through which professionals listen systemically for client needs in other component areas. When appropriate and with their consent, the staff introduce clients directly to other professionals. Personal introductions increase the potential for a successful referral (Bronfenbrenner, 1979).

Another advantage is that the model requires, but also helps maintain, a view of the "big picture." It forces professionals to think outside the "silo." For example, elder care is not just about putting an older adult somewhere to be cared for; it's about helping faculty and staff because they are people to whom family matters and who are valuable to the institution.

Adopting the model is one way that may allow for expanded program services and greater market penetration, even in the face of reduced financial support. Recruitment and retention efforts continue to demand nontraditional and creative strategies in a competitive global market. Adoption may also help reduce the rise of healthcare costs. Both academe and business share these challenges. There is also a desire to use the model to more effectively buffer campus communities from outside negative forces by having a larger and more widely connected internal presence. Such internal and external implications include reductions in force, site crisis events, and global disasters and conflicts.

Concerns

Having a supportive infrastructure for establishing a program similar to LWC is of paramount importance. The most tangible demonstration of this is a commitment to multiyear funding, and yet the interpersonal trust and understanding between administrators and program directors necessary for verbal and outspoken support is just as important.

Second, an integrated program will not succeed if there are "turf battles" and resistance to cooperation and collaboration. On the contrary, professionals must be able to "play" with ideas that relate to hybrid services. Assumptions about how components will operate may also lead to a blurring of boundaries. Details that must be clarified include confidentiality, information sharing and storage, and identifying gray areas in terms of scope of practices. An extension of this is the importance of practicing with integrity. Others in the institution must be able to trust that program providers will deliver utmost quality in services, be responsive to other units and departments, and be skilled and knowledgeable about each field and its community resources.

Strategies and Barriers

There is increasing interest in LWC's model and how it may be useful to other organizations. State-funded and private universities, a state agency, and companies in the nonprofit and for-profit sectors have discussed the adaptability of the model to their settings. Some are starting up entirely new programs; others are seeking to align existing programs. These experiences present strategies for and barriers to implementation that are worth noting.

Strategies

Build systemic partnerships with other campus entities. Colleges, departments, and constituency groups such as faculty, staff, and diversity organizations are all considered stakeholders and partners. The importance of this strategy cannot be understated. The reasons are twofold. The first is support, in which the campus community knows who the work–life unit is and values its activities. A strong base of support is essential, from both upper echelons of administration and midlevel management. The support of the latter is important because they will probably be the best conduit of marketing and referrals. The second reason is potential collaborations. Creating win–win scenarios with other campus units is a good way to influence the campus mesosystem and bring about culture change. Connectedness with other campus groups will determine the effectiveness of any systemic effort.

Regularly explore the trends and information at all levels: macrosystem, exosystem, and where possible, microsystems. This "future scanning" provides leads about how multiple systems may affect the institution and individual faculty and staff. By extension, these items may have an impact on future programming either by anticipating emerging needs or by steering clear of problems. For example, LWC's introduction of elder care more than 10 years ago, even before campus needs were articulated, came from awareness of changing demographics of an aging society and projected workforce elder care demands. Evolving definitions for family, dependents, and career will also continue to alter family-friendly work arrangements. These can include an increasing likelihood of career "ramp on/ramp off" work sequences (Hewlett & Luce, 2005), generally characterized by episodic workplace departures to address family needs, followed by returns to continue careers.

Establish a clear philosophy and mission statement. There is a fine line between providing services as a means of keeping people happy or doing the right thing and providing services because a systemic vision exists. The latter provides sustainable direction for the program and communicates purposefulness to the campus community.

Barriers

Be aware of the degree or lack of institutional buy-in. Without the knowledge and active support of entities such as risk management and safety, the campus health service, human resources, and others, establishing a sustainable program will be extremely difficult.

Accurately assess timing and resources when implementing or changing programs. Competing priorities within the institution, capacity problems, and duplicate services also can serve as barriers to establishing an effective program.

Make sure that the professionals operating the components being integrated are vested in the process and its sustainability. Lack of cooperation will cause the program to deteriorate into "silos," in which units work beside each other but do not work together.

Putting together a program such as LWC is a process that takes time. LWC has found that concerns about less than successful outcomes associated with the model appear to be related to unrealistic or inadequate structuring, rather than shortcomings in the model design. Actual need and resource availability must dictate what can be developed and when. Planners and managers should be wary of minimal supports or of potential failure when planned growth exceeds departmental and organizational means and capacity.

Conclusion

LWC has evolved into a systemic, multicomponent program guided and informed by the social ecology of health model. Empirical research and LWC practice suggests that this provides a valued, flexible, and informed approach for increasing faculty, staff, student, and institutional resiliency. There is similar potential for increased resiliency to other academic and nonacademic settings. Committed organizational sponsorship and engaged domain professionals, working thoughtfully and carefully, can develop services that effectively address whole-person issues and spillover between work and home while contouring them to their unique settings. The practice model described in this chapter offers useful, adaptable, and effective responses for addressing present and "next-generation" needs. Rapidly evolving university culture and climate changes, influenced by academic and global trends, will demand no less, now and in the future.

References

Attridge, M. (2005). The business case for the integration of employee assistance, work-life, and wellness services: A literature review. In M. Attridge, P. A. Herlihy, & R. P. Maiden (Eds.), *The integration of employee assistance, work/life, and wellness services* (pp. 31–56). Binghamton, NY: Haworth Press.

Attridge, M., Herlihy, P. A., & Maiden, R. P. (Eds.). (2005). *The integration of employee assistance, work/life, and wellness services.* Binghamton, NY: Haworth Press.

Bronfenbrenner, U. (1979). *The ecology of human development: Experiments by nature and design.* Cambridge, MA: Harvard University Press.

Bronfenbrenner, U., & Ceci, S. (1994). Nature-nurture reconceptualized in developmental perspective: A bioecological model. *Psychological Review, 101,* 568–586.

Burud, S., & Tumolo, M. (2004). *Leveraging the new human capital: Adaptive strategies, results achieved, and stories of transformation.* Palo Alto, CA: Davies-Black.

Frone, M., Russell, M., & Cooper, M. (1997). Relation of work-family conflict to health outcomes: A four-year longitudinal study of employed parents. *Journal of Occupational and Organizational Psychology, 70,* 325–335.

Grzywacz, J. (2000). Work-family spillover and health during midlife: Is managing conflict everything? *American Journal of Health Promotion, 14,* 236–243.

Grzywacz, J., Almeida, D., & McDonald, D. (2002). Work-family spillover and daily reports of work and family stress in the adult labor force. *Family Relations, 51,* 28–36.

Grzywacz, J., & Bass, B. (2003). Work, family, and mental health: Testing different models of work-family fit. *Journal of Marriage and Family, 65,* 248–262.

Grzywacz, J., & Carlson, D. (2007). Conceptualizing work–family balance: Implications for practice and research. *Advances in Developing Human Resources, 9*(4), 455–471.

Grzywacz, J., & Fuqua, J. (2000). The social ecology of health: Leverage points and linkages. *Behavioral Medicine, 26*(3), 101–115.

Grzywacz, J., & Marks, N. (2000a). Family, work, work-family spillover, and problem drinking during midlife. *Journal of Marriage and the Family, 62,* 336–348.

Grzywacz, J., & Marks, N. (2000b). Reconceptualizing the work-family interface: An ecological perspective on the correlates of positive and negative spillover between work and family. *Journal of Occupational Health Psychology 5*(1), 111–126.

Hammer, L., Cullen, J., Neal, M., Sinclair, R., & Shafiro, M. (2005). The longitudinal effects of work-family conflict and positive spillover on depressive symptoms among dual-earner couples. *Journal of Occupational Health Psychology, 10*(2), 138–154.

Herlihy, P. (2005). Perspectives on the future of integration. In M. Attridge, P. A. Herlihy, & R. P. Maiden (Eds.), *The integration of employee assistance, work/life, and wellness services* (pp. 407–418). Binghamton, NY: Haworth Press.

Hewlett, S. A., & Luce, C. B. (2005). Off-ramps and on-ramps: Keeping talented women on the road to success. *Harvard Business Review, 83*(3), 43–54.

Kolodny, A. (1998). Creating the family-friendly campus. In C. Coiner & D. H. George (Eds.), *The family track: Keeping your faculties while you mentor, nurture, teach, and serve* (pp. 284–310). Urbana: University of Illinois Press.

Norris, F., Stevens, S., Pfefferbaum, B., Wyche, K., & Pfefferbaum, R. (2008). Community resilience as a metaphor, theory, set of capabilities, and strategy for disaster readiness. *American Journal of Community Psychology, 41,* 127–150.

Pollard, W. (1996). *Soul of a firm.* New York: HarperBusiness/Zondervan.

Roman, P. (2005). A commentary on the integration of EAPs: Some cautionary notes from past and present. In M. Attridge, P. A. Herlihy, & R. P. Maiden (Eds.), *The integration of employee assistance, work/life, and wellness services* (pp. 395–406). Binghamton, NY: Haworth Press.

Sapolsky, R. (1999). *Why zebras don't get ulcers.* New York: Freeman.

Siebert, A. (1996). *Survivor personality.* New York: Berkley.

Sloan Work & Family Research Network. (n.d.). *Questions and answers about employer-supported child care: A Sloan Work & Family Research Network fact sheet.* Retrieved May 26, 2008, from http://www.bc.edu/wfnetwork

Sloan Work & Family Research Network. (2006). *Questions and answers about flexible work schedules: A Sloan Work & Family Research Network fact sheet.* Retrieved May 26, 2008, from http://www.bc.edu/wfnetwork

Stokols, D. (1996). Translating social ecology theory into guidelines for community health promotion. *American Journal of Health Promotion, 10*(4), 282–298.

Stokols, D., Pelletier, K., & Fielding, J. (1996). The ecology of work and health: Research and policy directions for the promotion of employee health. *Health Education Quarterly, 23*(2), 137–158.

Swihart, D., & Thompson, D. (2002). Successful program integration: An analysis of the challenges and opportunities facing an EAP that integrated with other programs reveals the keys to successfully serving the systemic needs of employees and work organizations. *EAP Association Exchange, 32*(5), 10–13.

Thomas, K. (2000). *Intrinsic motivation at work: Building energy and commitment.* San Francisco: Berrett-Koehler.

Thompson, D. A., & Swihart, D. L. (2005). University of Arizona Life & Work Connections: A synergistic strategy for maximizing whole-person productivity over the employees' life-cycle/work cycle. In M. Attridge, P. A. Herlihy, & R. P. Maiden (Eds.), *The integration of employee assistance, work/life, and wellness services* (pp. 105–121). Binghamton, NY: Haworth Press.

Wayne, J., Grzywacz, J., Carlson, D., & Kacmar, K. (2007). Work-family facilitation: A theoretical explanation and model of primary antecedents and consequences. *Human Resources Management Review, 17,* 63–76.

4

FAMILY-FRIENDLY POLICIES IN CATHOLIC COLLEGES AND UNIVERSITIES

A Socially Just Imperative

Jill Bickett and Emily Arms

Research on family-friendly policies in Catholic colleges and universities is long overdue. Though two important studies present findings about family-friendly policies across different institutional types (Hollenshead, Sullivan, Smith, August, & Hamilton, 2005; Wolf-Wendel & Ward, 2006), and other scholarship has focused on policy implementation exclusively at large research universities (Drago & Colbeck, 2003; Quinn, Lange, & Olswang, 2004; Wolf-Wendel & Ward, 2005), no studies have addressed the subset of Catholic colleges and universities that also employ large numbers of faculty. With the aging of the professoriate and the increasing numbers of young faculty entering university life seeking to balance work with parenthood, research across and within a wide variety of university contexts is necessary to determine where best practices in family-friendly policy can be found and how they may be best supported. This chapter is the first review of family-friendly policies at Catholic colleges and universities, and thus its scope and focus differ slightly from other reviews that have not exclusively addressed this unique institutional context.

The chapter begins with a brief explanation of the demographics of the colleges and universities we profile and the criteria for their selection. It continues with a discussion of the institutional context for the policy landscape at these universities, exploring mission and identity and how these elements may impact policy implementation. A brief overview of findings precedes the highlights of best-practice policies and their implementation at particular institutions, including passages from online materials available on college and university Web sites. Recommendations for family-friendly policy and practice conclude the chapter.

Policy and Mission

The Jesuit philosophy of "faith that does justice," which requires that all persons be treated with respect and dignity, is infused in the mission at each Jesuit institution (Jesuit Conference, 2008). This is a fitting institutional rationale for the adoption of best practices that provide for the care and nurture of faculty families. Catholic Jesuit colleges and universities are mission-driven institutions that advocate the "service of faith, in which the promotion of justice is an absolute requirement" (Jesuit Conference, 2008). This justice-oriented approach to mission influences "the kind of teaching, learning, and research that is pursued throughout the curriculum; the kind of caring relationships that are experienced in and out of the classroom; and the kind of values that permeate the institution" (Association of Jesuit Colleges and Universities, 2008). These values that permeate the institution should also extend to the formation of policy that meets the needs of faculty in some of their most important moments, such as when they bring life into the world or take care of a sick child or parent. Family-friendly policies seem well matched to the mission of the Jesuit university, but theory and practice may not always align. Intent and mission would dictate that Jesuit universities of all sizes would be some of the most family-friendly institutions in higher education. Yet a new hybrid—the Catholic, medium-sized, master's-granting college or university—may find it more challenging both financially and logistically to maintain the close ties to mission that its philosophy prescribes.

Neither small nor large, some of today's medium-sized Catholic universities find themselves in difficult middle ground. Although in various ways they are similar to the look and feel of smaller liberal arts colleges, many Catholic universities have grown in size over the last three decades, adding multiple graduate and professional programs that, according to the Carnegie Classification system, push them into the next category of a medium-sized, master's-granting university. Yet they lack the enrollment, doctoral program focus, and outside endowments of the larger research universities. Caught in the middle, medium-sized Catholic colleges and universities may retain vestiges of the small, family-like liberal arts college, but may also share characteristics with the larger comprehensive university.

Additional evidence that illustrates the conflicted "middle ground" of medium-sized Catholic colleges and universities is seen in how these schools identify themselves. This can be key to understanding the policy culture of the institution, but presents another challenge for the subset of Catholic institutions profiled in this chapter. Although the Carnegie system classifies each of our selected universities as medium master's-granting, each of these colleges or universities, by its own admission, has a dual identity rooted in a historical liberal arts tradition, but stretched to include the enlarged expectations of an institution with added enrollment and programmatic growth. For example, several of the medium master's-granting universities and colleges in our review refer to themselves as *liberal arts colleges,* which connotes the small, nurturing community of their past. In fact, Loyola College in Maryland, which is classified as a university, still retains the name *College* to emphasize the close-knit feel of its current academic community. This conflicted identity may manifest itself in the availability and application of family-friendly policies at these institutions. The literature on family-friendly policies that differentiates the liberal arts college from the larger, comprehensive university is instructive in understanding how to contextualize the policy landscape at this subset of colleges and universities.

Contextualizing the Policy Landscape

Though the research on family-friendly policies by institutional type is slim, several studies suggest that liberal arts colleges are uniquely family-friendly. Although research universities generally offer more benefits than masters-granting or liberal arts colleges (Hollenshead et al., 2005), the liberal arts college culture is characterized as a friendlier environment. The liberal arts college culture can provide a community feel where faculty are ensconced in a small, familylike atmosphere that supports and encourages both their personal and work life. In fact, Wolf-Wendel and Ward (2006) found that small liberal arts colleges, particularly the most elite and selective ones, tend to offer the most progressive family-friendly policies to their faculty, with most offering paid family leave benefits beyond the unpaid provisions of the federal

Family and Medical Leave Act. Wolf-Wendel and Ward further found that female faculty believed that the "family orientation of these colleges does help shape a more family-friendly environment in terms of policy" (p. 60). In addition, at liberal arts colleges where formal leave policies were more likely to be in place, faculty were less likely to have to negotiate their own leave, or arrange to cover their duties during their absence, and thus could focus on exploring more secondary needs such as childcare and family-friendly meeting times. However, despite a more friendly policy environment, obstacles for female faculty still exist at liberal arts colleges. Drago and Colbeck (2003) report that female faculty at teaching colleges delayed their academic careers in order to start a family, suggesting that accommodating family life, no matter how generous the environment, can still be problematic.

At comprehensive colleges and universities, which in program and degree conferral can be comparable to the medium master's-granting Catholic institutions, family-friendly policies were limited, less clear, and not as readily accessible to faculty (Drago & Colbeck, 2003; Wolf-Wendel & Ward, 2006). Wolf-Wendel and Ward (2006) found that faculty at comprehensive colleges and universities lived in a state of uncertainty because of the extremely informal nature of the policy context. Some faculty at these universities were unaware of what family-friendly policies were available to them. At these institutions, faculty were focused on acquiring the proper leave and finding someone to teach their courses during their absence, because adjunct professors were generally unavailable. They had little time to negotiate other benefits that might be available, such as stopping the tenure clock or modifying duties for a family leave. Indeed, compared to liberal arts colleges, the comprehensive university is generally one where much work has still to be done on the work and family policy front (Wolf-Wendel & Ward, 2006). Thus although larger schools such as the comprehensive university may have more resources for policy implementation, they may also be more bureaucratic, making policies less flexible and more inaccessible for faculty (Drago & Colbeck, 2003).

Catholic, medium-sized, master's-granting institutions are a new breed, similar in some ways to liberal arts colleges because of their family feel, yet in some ways comparable to the public comprehensive colleges where the policy environment is less formal and faculty must work hard to access and implement the family-friendly policies available to them. The middle ground that these Catholic colleges and universities inhabit produces a unique, though perhaps challenging policy landscape.

Selection Criteria and Demographics

We selected the universities for our review based on three criteria: (1) Catholic affiliation, (2) medium-sized master's-granting, and (3) policies available. We began by using the template for family-friendly policies suggested by Hollenshead and colleagues (2005) in their Faculty Work/Family Policy Study undertaken by the Center for the Education of Women at the University of Michigan. These policies included but were not limited to tenure clock stop, modified duties, and paid leave benefits. These three broad policy categories also aligned with the "three cornerstone family accommodation policies" as defined by the UC Faculty Family Friendly Edge (Mason, Goulden, & Wolfinger, 2006).

Each institution that we profiled was required to have one of the three "cornerstone" policies available and accessible online for its faculty. Thus, though not a purposeful selection, the Catholic colleges that met the stated criteria and were therefore included in our review were all Jesuit affiliated (see Table 4.1).

TABLE 4.1
Profile of Selected Colleges and Universities based on the Carnegie Classification System

University	Enrollment (Fall 2004)	Graduate Instructional Program
Canisius College	5,018	Postbaccalaureate/professional
Creighton University	6,722	Doctoral, professions dominant
John Carroll University	4,101	Postbaccalaureate comprehensive
Loyola College	6,156	Doctoral, professions dominant
Loyola Marymount University	8,770	Postbaccalaureate comprehensive
University of Scranton	4,795	Postbaccalaureate with arts and sciences

It is not enough for universities to simply offer family-friendly policies. Benefits and policies must be accessible as well. With that in mind, the universities profiled had to have all policies detailed in their online resources to be considered for inclusion in our review. Research has shown that policies that are not written are less clear and more open to variant interpretations, causing inequitable implementation within the university (Gappa, Austin, & Trice, 2007). Further, policies that are not online are less easily accessible and less likely to be used by faculty. This may seem to be a minimum standard for all universities; however, we found that many of the Catholic institutions surveyed either did not have policies online or required special password codes to access policy or benefit information. In addition to eliciting information on the policies online, we conducted telephone interviews and e-mail communications with university representatives.

Highlighting Policies and Additional Benefits

As we explored the policy landscape at our chosen Catholic Jesuit colleges and universities, we discovered some interesting findings related to the three "cornerstone" policy categories we had selected; however, we also found other distinct benefits that lay outside these specific domains. Therefore we broadened our definition of family-friendly policies to include categories such as tuition and housing assistance and childcare and lactation facilities. Helping families afford housing and college tuition and providing quality childcare and lactation facilities are also policies that should be considered under the family-friendly umbrella.

Our original intent was to find one or two institutions that had a multitude of family-friendly policies and to highlight these colleges or universities as exemplary. Although some of the institutions had excellent policies, none had every benefit that we identified. For example, one institution had a substantial paid leave policy, but did not offer childcare. Another had substantial childcare accommodations but no paid leave. In addition, we were reluctant to laud schools as exemplary if they did not have all three of the cornerstone family accommodations, which we acknowledge were developed by the University of California for large research institutions. Smaller institutions may find it difficult to provide certain types of benefits for various reasons. This may be why the middle ground of medium-sized Catholic colleges and universities is particularly challenging. Thus, instead of highlighting specific institutions, we note exemplary policies that individual colleges and universities have in place.

Overview of Policies in Catholic Jesuit Universities

Five of the six institutions offered paid leave policies, and all but one included language in the faculty handbook about extending the probationary period. No schools had language in the faculty handbook about active service modified duties (ASMD), though representatives from several schools said that these decisions would be made on a case-by-case basis. Two schools provided on-campus childcare, and one had an off-site affiliation with another college for faculty childcare. Three mentioned lactation accommodations in online policies, and all had tuition remission programs. Three schools discussed housing assistance in their online materials. Following is a discussion of specific family-friendly policies—leave policies, extended probationary time, tuition assistance, housing assistance, childcare, and lactation accommodations—that serve as best practices for Catholic institutions.

Best-Practice Policies at Catholic Jesuit Universities

Leave Policies

Although leave policies are the most complex and perhaps the most expensive benefit that universities can offer, five of the six institutions provide some form of paid leave to their faculty for childbirth. In light of research that illustrates how paid pregnancy leave results in better health outcomes for mothers and children (Institute for Women's Policy Research, 2007), this best practice is clearly in line with the Jesuit mission to "value the dignity of human life" (Jesuit Conference, 2008). Loyola College in Maryland, in particular, offers an excellent paid pregnancy leave policy that is unique in both its content and clarity (see Exhibit 4.1).

Loyola College's policy language, which allows "up to a maximum of one semester," is an exemplary family-friendly accommodation because the paid leave and benefits run concurrently with the faculty semester time frame. Faculty do not have to worry about financial arrangements for covering the portion of leave unpaid by the university. Other Catholic universities offer paid leave benefits of 6 to 12 weeks, but none have language that allows this generous semester-long paid leave.

EXHIBIT 4.1
Policy for Faculty Parental Leave at
Loyola College in Maryland

Tenured and tenure-track faculty, *without regard to length of service,* may apply for one semester of *paid* parental leave due to the birth or adoption of a child, or the assignment of a foster child. Such leave may only be taken during the first year of birth, adoption, or assignment.

Full-time affiliate and four-fifths-time faculty members with at least one year of service with the College may apply for one semester of *paid* parental leave due to the birth or adoption of a child, or the assignment of a foster child. Such leave may only be taken during the first year of birth, adoption, or assignment.

The faculty member on parental leave will have no teaching duties during the semester in which he or she is on leave. In addition, the faculty member is not required to participate in the life of the College or the department during the first 12 weeks of parental leave. However, depending on departmental needs as determined by the Department Chair and Dean, the faculty member may be expected to participate in the life of the Department, the College, and professionally at the end of the 12 weeks.

If all or part of a faculty member's parental leave qualifies as FMLA leave, time taken as parental leave will run concurrently with any FMLA leave. *Salary* and College paid benefits will continue for the duration of the leave up to a maximum of one semester.

Source: http://www.loyola.edu/academics/academicaffairs/documents/FH% 2007.pdf (retrieved May 3, 2008).

Further, allowing paid leave "without regard to length of service" is a significant benefit. Newly hired faculty may choose to start a family and need to immediately use family paid leave. Allowing immediate access to this benefit can make a difference in recruiting and retaining quality faculty. The message is not, "We want to reward you for staying here," but rather, "We want to keep you here." Clear paid leave policies of this length with generous eligibility requirements can alleviate the "fear factor" (Ward & Wolf-Wendel, 2007) that causes some faculty to avoid using campus policies related to having a child, for fear of being perceived as not serious about a faculty career. Extending the benefit to full-time affiliates and four-fifths-time faculty is also an unusual benefit and very family-friendly.

In addition, Loyola College does not discriminate by gender in the application of the leave policy. If the spouse of the primary caretaker is a faculty member but chooses to take leave to bond with the new child and share in parenting duties, he or she will be supported by the university in this choice. The policy also specifically sets out job expectations during leave, another important anxiety-reducing policy. Transparency, generous paid leave without regard to length of service, and a commitment to both genders in the implementation of the leave policy make Loyola College's parental leave policy one to emulate.

Policies That Extend the Probationary Period

Five of the six universities offer faculty members the option of extending their probationary time to tenure, sometimes called stopping the tenure clock. The use of a pause in the tenure clock provides faculty time to adjust to the new demands of parenting after childbirth or adoption without jeopardizing their chances at tenure. Although the implementation of this benefit varies little, it has some interesting features to consider, though again the detail of the policy and transparency that is provided to faculty most benefits them. The policy at the University of Scranton serves as a good example of these benefits (see Exhibit 4.2).

The detail in the probation extension policy at the University of Scranton provides the most important benefit: transparency. When faculty know the policies, understand that they are entitlements, and know that they do not require individual negotiation, they are more likely to feel that there is no stigma attached to using them (Hollenshead et al., 2005). Further, language that states that birth or adoption by "a faculty member or the spouse of a faculty member" suggests that the University of Scranton also does not discriminate by gender in the application of this benefit, allowing more than the primary caregiver to take the time to bond with the new child. Being specific about the nature and timing of evaluative reviews during the tenure extension clarifies faculty expectations, and indicating in writing that faculty will be evaluated for tenure as if no postponement had occurred is an important assurance that faculty deserve when making the tenure extension decision.

EXHIBIT 4.2
Policy for Extension of the Probationary Period
at the University of Scranton

Upon the birth of a child or the adoption of a child under the age of six by a faculty member or the spouse of a faculty member, the date of the faculty member's tenure review will be postponed by one year. Within one year of the birth or adoption, but in no case later than November of the year of the scheduled tenure review, the faculty member will write to the Provost/VPAA [vice president of academic affairs] to confirm or decline the one-year postponement. Failing to submit such timely notification will constitute a *de facto* rejection of the extension.

   No more than two such postponements may occur for any faculty member. Reappointment/non-reappointment reviews will take place annually. . . . The criteria for the tenure evaluation of the faculty member will be the same as if no postponement had occurred.

Source: http://academic.scranton.edu/organization/fac/handbook/Faculty_Handbook.pdf (retrieved May 3, 2008).

Tuition Assistance

All six of the Jesuit colleges and universities had tuition remission programs for spouses and dependent children of faculty members. Not all private universities offer this type of benefit. However, because the principal work of the Jesuit order is education, offering substantial tuition remission programs aligns well with its continuing mission. The Jesuits are to be commended for their commitment to the education of employees and their families. This family-friendly policy can continue to benefit faculty throughout their lifetime. The language in the Canisius College handbook is a good representation of the policy considerations related to this benefit (see Exhibit 4.3).

   After 3 years of employment, faculty dependents and spouses may receive 100% tuition remission, and Canisius College will consider allowing previous employment to count toward this 3-year service requirement. Though one may not immediately think of providing education for the spouses and dependents of faculty when considering family-friendly policies, these can be low-cost benefits that make a difference for faculty over the life span of their career.

EXHIBIT 4.3
Policy for Tuition Remission at Canisius College

The College will waive tuition charges for undergraduate study, over and above the amount of all applicable state, federal, or private scholarship awards, for children to age 30 and spouses of full-time faculty members, based on the following schedule of full-time service: upon employment, 25% waiver; first anniversary, 50% waiver; second anniversary, 75% waiver; third anniversary, 100% waiver. Prior full-time employment in institutions of higher education will be counted toward fulfilling the required service factor. . . .

If a faculty member dies, or suffers 100% disability while in service to the College, or has retired, the surviving dependent children and spouse are also eligible for these waivers.

Source: http://www.canisius.edu/images/userImages/chuckp/Page_10333 faculty_handbook_2007.pdf (retrieved May 3, 2008).

In addition, all universities belong to a Jesuit program called the Faculty Children Exchange Program (FACHEX), which allows the children of faculty, administrators, and staff at one Jesuit college to receive tuition remission at another participating Jesuit college. Five of the six universities also participated in Tuition Exchange, Inc. (TE), which is a reciprocal scholarship program for children and other family members of faculty at participating universities. Both the University of Scranton and John Carroll University participated in three tuition exchange programs: FACHEX, TE, and the Council of Independent Colleges (CIC-TEP).

Housing Assistance

Families need a place to call home. A true family-friendly university understands this. In the current faculty hiring climate, faculty are often required to move great distances to secure teaching appointments in their selected field. Moving across the country to an unknown region can cause significant upheaval in the life of a family. Providing benefits that make this transition easier is a family-friendly initiative aligned with the Catholic emphasis on the importance of family in today's society. Housing assistance can be an important recruiting tool for new faculty in a time of escalating real estate prices. Assistance in the form of forgivable loans was offered by three of the six universities, but the program at Loyola Marymount University in Los Angeles was the most generous (see Exhibit 4.4).

In order for housing assistance to be a true benefit, the amount of financial assistance offered must align with the prices of the housing market near the university. Loyola Marymount University (LMU) in Los Angeles, an expensive housing market, offers a $100,000 forgivable loan to faculty as long as they remain employed at LMU for the duration of the loan. A representative from the university indicated that nine faculty in the last fiscal year had taken advantage of this policy. Allowing faculty to purchase housing within 50 miles of the campus is also a significant benefit and may permit families to choose housing that provides a convenient commute for more than one family member. The LMU representative also indicated that though not on the Web site, rental assistance was available to faculty on a sliding scale based on family size and salary.

Childcare

A 2003 study of professors in the University of California system found that on-campus childcare was the most important "family-friendly resource" that the university could provide for faculty (Mason, Stacy, & Goulden, 2003). The presence of an on-campus childcare facility sends a clear message to faculty that childcare is an important part of meeting the needs of the whole

---

EXHIBIT 4.4
Policy for Housing Assistance at
Loyola Marymount University

New faculty are eligible to participate in the Housing Assistance Plan after their first year (e.g., the program goes into effect with the second year contract). The program contains some of the following elements:

- No cap on household income for eligibility
- Loan for a down payment up to $100,000
- The new home may be located within 50 miles of campus

Source: http://www.lmu.edu/Page41443.aspx (retrieved May 3, 2008).

family, not just the needs of the individual faculty member—a family-friendly approach in line with the Jesuit mission. Two of the institutions offer on-campus infant/childcare and a third college offers a partnership with a local childcare provider. Creighton University provides on-campus, high-quality childcare to the campus community. Information about the childcare center can be found both in the faculty handbook and on a Web site devoted to the center (see Exhibit 4.5).

Having an accessible and extensive Web site goes beyond the minimum requirement for transparency and accessibility. Often childcare centers are tucked away on campuses, and new faculty may be unaware of their existence and reluctant to ask. Having significant material online, including information on philosophy, curriculum, goals, parent councils, and fees can be both

---

EXHIBIT 4.5
Philosophy of the Child Development Center
at Creighton University

The Creighton University Child Development Center provides the nurturing essential to the emotional, social, intellectual, and physical growth of the child. The care and education of the child is based upon a partnership between the Center and the family. The Center is committed to supporting each family and the family's goal for the child. The teachers hold a sacred respect for the child, which serves as the foundation for the care routines and curriculum.

The Jesuit tradition of service to others is a key element in the social norm of the Center. Caregivers, parents, and students are dedicated to the concept of responsibility to the community and to the world.

The Center is accredited through the National Association for the Education of Young Children (NAEYC) Academy for Early Childhood Program Accreditation. Programs that are accredited have voluntarily undergone a comprehensive process of internal self-study, invited an external professional review to verify compliance with the Criteria for High Quality Early Childhood Programs, and have been in substantial compliance with the Criteria.

Source: http://www2.creighton.edu/adminfinance/childdevelopmentcenter/philosophycurriculumgoals/index.php (retrieved May 3, 2008).

a recruiting and retention tool. Further, accreditation by the National Association for the Education of Young Children (NAEYC) is an exemplary practice that assures faculty of consistent high-quality care for their children. Not all university childcare centers are accredited. Enrollment for children at Creighton's childcare center is available to infants as young as 6 weeks, which is particularly helpful for the new faculty parent who may want to return to work quickly, but also wants to have the new child nearby on campus. Also at Creighton, though faculty pay a fee, tuition is competitive with surrounding daycare facilities. According to a school representative, because tuition does not cover the cost of running the facility, the university subsidizes 20% of the program over what the fees cover.

An option for institutions that cannot offer an on-campus facility is to partner with neighboring institutions that have childcare facilities. One university had an off-campus affiliation with another nearby college daycare center. Another university was set to begin a childcare voucher program for 10% of the average cost of childcare in the university's surrounding area. All of the universities offered childcare referral services for faculty, though none had Web site access to this information.

Lactation Accommodations

Unlike childcare facilities, lactation accommodations may cost the university little but can do much to show particular support to female faculty members. Of the six universities, three offer lactation accommodations, with Loyola College in Maryland providing the most comprehensive information on the accommodation. Its dedicated "Mother's Room" on campus has its own Web site, which includes a mission statement in alignment with a family-friendly campus (see Exhibit 4.6).

The language used in this mission statement is clear and the use of the room is described without euphemism, revealing an acceptance and comfort level with lactation accommodations that was not revealed at any other university. Further, the Web site is specific about how to use the room and how to negotiate access, including acquisition of keys, sign-up sheets, and room maintenance. The university provides a hospital-grade pump for all lactating mothers. These amenities go far beyond the informal practice of simply offering an empty room for the breast-feeding mother.

EXHIBIT 4.6
Policy on Reserved Lactation Accommodations
at Loyola College in Maryland
Mission Statement

The Mother's Room was established to support working families at Loyola College. This Room is a quiet, peaceful space to let breast-feeding mothers express the milk their infants need for healthy development.

Source: http://www.loyola.edu/HR/Benefits/Additional%20Resources/The MothersRoom (retrieved May 3, 2008).

Recommendations for Best Practice

Our inability to deem any medium-sized Jesuit Catholic university as exemplary may be a consequence of the challenging middle ground in which they reside. The university policies that we highlight, however, are good examples of what can be accomplished when resources and university administration support a mission and philosophy that are the driving force behind a strong family-friendly policy environment. Based on these six institutions' policies and programs, we offer the following recommendations to Catholic institutions and other medium-sized colleges that wish to assist employees with work-family balance.

Make Policies Transparent

Although some policies can be expensive endeavors for universities, others are just good practice that can cost little. Formalizing policies and making them easily accessible is a low-cost remedy that can do a great deal to lower faculty anxiety by making transparent what is available at each institution. This reduces the fear factor for faculty who may be afraid to inquire because of administrative perception about their academic devotion. Lack of easy online public access to family-friendly policies may create an environment where faculty believe they must negotiate separate deals for individual circumstances. Proliferation of individual deals may create inequitable application of policy across the university and could expose institutions to legal liability for preferential treatment of one employee over another. It is simply good business to be up front about all family-friendly policies or the lack of them.

Catholic universities that pride themselves on a "family atmosphere" cannot be true to their mission if they are willing to treat individual faculty members in an inequitable way. More specifically, Jesuit universities that advocate for "promotion of justice" and "dignity of human life" cannot be fully compliant with their mission unless they provide faculty with information for families who are bringing new life into the world. Transparency and access are the cornerstones to the promotion of social justice.

Offer Paid Leave

Expensive benefits such as paid leave may be difficult for some medium-sized Catholic universities that, because of financial constraints, are forced to choose which accommodations they may offer. Paid leave in these types of universities is an exemplary benefit because few schools have it. It represents a conscious choice on the part of the institution to devote funding to the support of the families who have made the commitment to caring for a new child. This again is in concert with the justice focus of the Jesuit order. However, even if paid leave is not a possibility for some Catholic universities, state-funded paid family leave can provide a portion of faculty salary during leave. However, this benefit is not yet available in every state. Universities should be proactive in advocating for state legislation that can help employees replace salary during family leave, as it may lessen the financial responsibility of the university and free up funds for implementation of other family-friendly benefits. Further, best practice would require that eligibility for paid leave be immediate on university employment.

Extend the Tenure Clock

Another low-cost remedy that all Catholic universities should adopt is the extension of the probationary period. This is a no-cost benefit that can significantly improve the life circumstances of pre-tenure faculty who start families after beginning their tenure-track appointment. It clearly addresses the Jesuit philosophy to acknowledge the whole person, not just the employee of the university. Language in the policy that states that extending the probationary period will not negatively affect a faculty member's chances of gaining tenure is also recommended. Again, this policy allows faculty in difficult transitional periods to more effectively balance work and life and to feel secure that upheavals in personal life can be managed without a negative impact on their professional life. The access and transparency of this policy is imperative because faculty fear is greatest in this pre-tenure period. Being clear about university policy and not having to ask about or negotiate the stopping of the tenure clock should be an entitlement for all faculty.

Introduce a Reduction in Teaching Duties Following Major Life Events

Active service modified duties (ASMD) allows faculty to adjust their teaching load to accommodate family needs such as child or elder care. Though none of the institutions offered this benefit, they were clearly aware that it could be important. The Jesuit mandate that advocates for protecting the dignity of all persons is the perfect rationale for this benefit, and yet none of the colleges or universities had formalized this policy for their faculty, suggesting that the alignment of mission and practice can sometimes be inconsistent. Departmental hiring of adjunct professors provides faculty the flexibility to gradually resume work responsibilities, sometimes without a commensurate reduction in pay. Several university representatives reported that this practice took place on a case-by-case basis. University funding for adjunct professors provides a twofold advantage to the faculty. It allows departments to more easily offer modified duty, and it also ensures that other faculty will not be burdened by the extra workload created by the leave. Also, in tandem with providing ASMD may be the possibility of offering more flexible career paths such as part-time tenure track, clinical faculty positions, and research-only positions.

Provide Access to Quality Childcare

On-campus childcare is also a difficult enterprise for some universities, and even more difficult is subsidizing this benefit. Offsetting the cost of an accredited on-campus childcare facility so that employees do not have to pay exorbitant prices is an exemplary practice that can alleviate some of the financial burden for new families. If on-campus childcare is not financially feasible for the university, other benefits may be provided that can help in this regard. Offering childcare reimbursement vouchers is one way that universities can support families with children. Seeking out neighborhood institutions or other colleges for childcare provider affiliations is another possible solution. Providing accessible, online, well-researched, accredited childcare and babysitting referrals should be a best practice for all universities. Childcare is rooted in the Jesuit philosophy of holding sacred the dignity of the individual and providing care for the whole person. Accommodating the children of faculty is a mission-driven practice that should be a priority on all Jesuit Catholic campuses.

Conclusion

Perhaps no medium-sized Catholic university can afford all of these policies, but small important steps can be taken to improve family-friendly policy accommodations. Faculty devoted to the unique mission of the Catholic university deserve no less. The mission and philosophy of Catholic universities provides them with a social justice imperative to dedicate appropriate attention and resources toward their family-friendly policy accommodations. More must be done to fund research and complete studies that can provide an expansive and in-depth understanding of this unique educational policy context so that the social justice imperative for Catholic universities can be properly and wholly met.

References

Association of Jesuit Colleges and Universities (AJCU). (2008). Retrieved February 28, 2008, from http://www.ajcunet.edu

Canisius College. (2007). *Faculty handbook: Further benefits* (chap. 9b). Retrieved May 3, 2008, from http://www.canisius.edu/images/userImages/chuckp/Page_10333/faculty_handbook_2007.pdf

Creighton University. (n.d.). *Child development center: Philosophy and goals.* Retrieved May 3, 2008, from http://www2.creighton.edu/adminfinance/child developmentcenter/philosophycurriculumgoals/index.php

Drago, R., & Colbeck, C. (2003). *The mapping project: Exploring the terrain of U.S. colleges and universities for faculty and families.* University Park: Pennsylvania State University.

Gappa, J., Austin, A., & Trice, A. (2007). *Rethinking faculty work: Higher education's strategic imperative.* San Francisco: Wiley.

Hollenshead, C. S., Sullivan, B., Smith, G. C., August, L., & Hamilton, S. (2005). Work/family policies in higher education: Survey data and case studies of policy implementation. In J. W. Curtis (Ed.), *The challenge of balancing faculty careers and family work: New directions for higher education, no. 130* (pp. 41–65). San Francisco: Jossey-Bass.

Institute for Women's Policy Research. (2007). *Fact sheet: Maternity leave in the United States.* Retrieved March 30, 2008, from http://www.iwpr.org/pdf/parental leaveA131.pdf

Jesuit Conference. (2008). *What makes a Jesuit school Jesuit? The relationship between Jesuit schools and the Society of Jesus.* Retrieved April 5, 2008, from http://www .jesuit.org/JesuitSchools/WhatMakesAJesuitSchoolJesuit/default.aspx

Loyola College in Maryland. (2007). *Faculty handbook: Faculty parental leave* (VII-12a). Retrieved May 3, 2008, from http://www.loyola.edu/academics/academic affairs/documents/FH%2007.pdf

Loyola College in Maryland. (n.d.). *Human resources: The mother's room.* Retrieved May 3, 2008, from http://www.loyola.edu/HR/Benefits/Additional%20 Resources/TheMothersRoom

Loyola Marymount University. *Real estate and faculty housing.* (n.d.) Retrieved May 3, 2008, from http://www.lmu.edu/Page41443.aspx

Mason, M. A., Goulden, M. & Wolfinger, N. (2006). Babies matter: Pushing the gender equity revolution forward. In S. J. Bracken, J. K. Allen, & D. R. Dean (Eds.), *The balancing act: Gendered perspectives in faculty roles and work lives* (pp. 9–29). Sterling, VA: Stylus.

Mason, M. A., Stacy, A., & Goulden, M. (2003). *The UC faculty work and family survey.* University of California, Berkeley. Retrieved April 9, 2008, from http:// ucfamilyedge.berkeley.edu

Quinn, K., Lange, S., & Olswang, S. (2004). Family-friendly policies and the research university. *Academe, 90,* 32–34.

University of Scranton. (2006). *Faculty handbook: Probationary period* (21.3). Retrieved May 3, 2008, from http://academic.scranton.edu/organization/fac/ handbook/Faculty_Handbook.pdf

Ward, K., & Wolf-Wendel, L. (2007). Managing work and family on the tenure track. *Teachers College Record,* May 17, 2007. Retrieved January 14, 2008, from http://www.tcrecord.org/content.asp?contentid = 14491

Wolf-Wendel, L., & Ward, K. (2005). Policy contexts for work and family: Perspectives from research university faculty. In J. W. Curtis (Ed.), *The challenge of balancing faculty careers and family work: New directions for higher education, no. 130* (pp. 67–80). San Francisco: Jossey-Bass.

Wolf-Wendel, L., & Ward, K. (2006). Faculty work and family life: Policy perspectives from different institutional types. In S. J. Bracken, J. K. Allen, & D. R. Dean (Eds.), *The balancing act: Gendered perspectives in faculty roles and work lives* (pp. 51–72). Sterling, VA: Stylus.

5

HOPKINS 24/7

The Story of Leadership and Excellence in Work and Personal Life

Kathleen Beauchesne

L
ike other organizations, universities and academic medical centers are not immune to workforce problems. Increasingly, leaders in institutions of higher education are finding it more and more difficult to carry out their mission in the face of social, economic, and demographic shifts. Institutions of higher education and academic medicine also are finding that they must respond to the impact of technology, distance learning, changes in funding patterns for education and research, and health care reform. In addition, higher education is feeling increased pressure for inclusion and sensitivity from diverse workforces and student populations and increased competition from the corporate sector, especially from progressive corporation-developed work–life programs and policies. The burden of these societal stresses and strains on leaders in higher education was aptly summed up by one senior executive who joined a committee to address work–life issues: "When I joined this committee, I expected that we would make recommendations for a new childcare program or something like that. What I learned was the issues we are facing are far more complex and will require much more of us to resolve." Simply put, the changes in work and family life over the past 30 years have been dramatic, and understanding the social issues that drive the formation of work–life programs and services demands the best thinking of all of us.

Today, hospitals and universities are seeking innovative ways to reach out to their employees; to support them in their personal lives, as parents, and as family members; and to address the new realities of the labor market and the shifting economic landscape. Given these trends, it is essential that all institutions of higher learning understand the relationship between an individual's work and personal life. This work–life relationship involves numerous issues, many of which, such as access to paid time off, workplace flexibility, and retirement and pensions, resist straightforward resolution. For example, to achieve true flexibility at work, managers and supervisors must be willing to give up the idea of "face time" and change their management styles and practices, which often requires management training. Plus, retirement is no longer the singular gold-watch event it once was. 401(k) and 403(b) plans have replaced pensions. Now, employees must make multiple financial decisions and consult with financial advisors to plan for retirement.

This chapter describes the work of the Office of WORKlife Programs at the Johns Hopkins Institutions (JHI) in Baltimore, Maryland, providing an account of its leadership work, in partnership with colleagues, to assess the trends mentioned previously using integrated models of service delivery. The chapter begins with a brief history of the work–life movement at Johns Hopkins and focuses on the ways in which a series of initiatives helped change the organizational culture to one that recognized the need to help faculty and staff balance their personal and professional responsibilities. Using John Kotter's (1995) eight steps for organizational change, the chapter outlines the changes that the institution underwent before concluding with suggestions for others interested in introducing similar organizational change on their own campuses.

Background: About Johns Hopkins and WORKlife Programs

The JHI consists of the Johns Hopkins University (JHU) and Johns Hopkins Hospital and Health System (JHHS), which is a separate corporation. With nine schools, JHU enrolls nearly 20,000 students on three campuses in Baltimore, Washington, D.C., and Montgomery County, Maryland, and in a variety of locations throughout the Baltimore–Washington area and at satellite campuses in China and Italy. Both the university and the hospital have grown considerably since the early days of WORKlife Programs. JHI now employs about 37,000 individuals and is one of Maryland's largest private employers. JHI seeks to employ highly educated and skilled professionals; as the baby boomers near retirement, JHI (like many universities) faces a dwindling supply of people with such qualifications.

Work–life concerns have been addressed by a variety of offices at JHU. In 1986, the hospital and university joined together to develop the Faculty and Staff Assistance Program (FASAP), an employee assistance program (EAP) intended to maximize human potential and to facilitate organizational improvement (Ginsberg, Kilburg, & Gomes, 1994, 1999). FASAP's services were extended not only to employees, but also to their family members—a unique and unusual approach for an EAP in the mid-1980s. FASAP was a success in helping workers with a variety of personal and work-related problems. However, childcare was beyond its purview and was outsourced.

The vice president of human resources and FASAP leadership, however, believed that an enhanced internal service program would best serve Hopkins employees. In response, the hospital and university established WORKlife Programs during the 1992–1993 academic year, with the specific goal of addressing childcare and elder care resources and referrals. The first task of WORKlife Programs was to provide childcare resources and referrals to all employees and students; the next was to develop elder care services for an aging workforce. Within a few years, the program was ranked one of the top 29 programs in a study by the Families and Work Institute and the CUPA Foundation (Friedman, Rimsky, & Johnson, 1996). This honor (and others) was achievable only because leadership was stable over two decades and through careful interpretation and adherence to organizational change, systems, and life span developmental theories.

In addition to its leadership and organizational work, WORKlife Programs and its five-member staff maintained a comprehensive program of work–life services for all faculty and staff in the university and hospital, including a dependent-care consultation and referral service; diverse support groups for faculty and staff; the Earned Income Tax Credit Campaign; a life span financial planning and retirement education program; the Live Near Your Work Program; a relocation assistance program; and subsidized sick, emergency, and backup care programs. Other programs included dependent-care subsidy and financial assistance programs; ongoing support groups, educational workshops, seminars on a variety of topics, and work–life training for leadership development and supervisors; and flexible scheduling training for supervisors. Although the model was unique because of its attention to collaboration and comprehensive focus, it provided a standard set of work–life services that can be found on many campuses around the country.

Unlike many other similar programs of its kind, WORKlife Programs coordinated its efforts with other human services programs and used an integrated operating structure to achieve its goals. Practitioners and researchers in the EAP and work–life industry have long advocated integration as cost effective because of the similarities in structure of the different programs. For example, all such programs require systems for intake and follow-up, have databases of referral resources, and offer core consultation services to employees, managers, and supervisors. Other organizations also have integrated these types of programs for the ease of service to employees, offering "one-stop shopping" for work–life, EAP, and health and wellness (see Attridge, 2005; Attridge & Gornick, 2003; Beidel, 2005; Bidgood, Boudewyn, & Fasbinder, 2005; Ginsberg et al., 1994, 1999; Gornick & Blair, 2005; Herlihy & Attridge, 2005; Thompson & Swihart, 2005; Turner, Weiner, & Keegan, 2005).

The Office of Human Services: An Integrated Model of Human Resources Development

Drawing on industry trends and supported by this literature on integrated work–life, EAPs, and behavioral health and wellness programs, an integrated model of employee assistance, work–life, and student assistance was put together in 1997 under the Office of Human Services (OHS). Ginsberg and colleagues (1994, 1999) discuss the advantages of providing EAP and other human services in an organizational and systems context and describe the model developed by OHS at Hopkins. Integrating human services programs was viewed as a way to provide a more comprehensive and systemic approach to individual, departmental, and broader organizational issues. Within this environment of integrated human resources development, the Office of WORKlife Programs was one of five service units comprising the OHS model. The other service programs were the Career Management Program (CMP), the Faculty and Staff Assistance Program (FASAP), Organizational Development and Diversity (OD&D), and the Center for Training and Education (T&E). OHS reported to the vice president of human resources. The OHS model was developed based on general systems theory, and the systems approach was designed to support the wide-ranging needs of a complex, modern organization like JHI. The OHS model served as a foundation for organizational and leadership change for more than 20 years. The conviction that human services work in universities could not be accomplished in isolation created an organizational climate of creativity and change that enabled WORKlife Programs, FASAP, and Student Assistance to later integrate their operations in response to industry trends and research.

The integrated OHS model supports the idea that universities and academic medical centers are a network of communities encompassing a complicated system of interrelated parts. Although each of the programs assisted faculty, staff, and their families in coping with personal problems and managing their careers, thus improving the resilience and stress hardiness of the psychosocial foundation of the university, the human services framework facilitated organizational improvement and change and the evolution of an inclusive organizational culture and expanded the knowledge and skill base of faculty and staff. Furthermore, the conceptual framework was consistent with lifespan models of human development (Ginsberg et al, 1994, 1999), a concept well known to the work–life field. Because the OHS model involves systemic analysis and organizational assessment in planning and delivering such interventions, the timing of the interventions and the use of existing committees, teams, task forces, policy initiatives, and other organizational modes commonly used in universities is important as well as the impact across the life span of the person, the person's family, the work team, other related organizational units, leadership, and the organization as a whole.

This integrated framework led to a series of organizational interventions on critical work–life issues, which expanded the opportunity for the organizational leadership work described here. Using the strategies for change described next, JHI took action to embed work–life issues into the culture of the institution.

Leading Change: Lessons Learned

In 1995, John Kotter published his research on 100 companies and their efforts to change in the *Harvard Business Review*. He found that organizational change is a process and outlined eight steps for leading change. He states that each step builds on the others, and that to be successful, none can be skipped. Kotter's research and his eight steps, which follow, guided the organizational efforts of WORKlife Programs.

Step 1: Establish a Sense of Urgency

Over the past 20 years, the issues that drove the work–life agenda were demographic, social, political, and economic, national issues that are still being debated yet today. The importance of each has been described throughout this chapter, but their importance also is defined by national crises, such as the events of 9/11, the war in Iraq, and violence on campus. These external factors, combined with the internal situations and needs that arose within JHI, created pressure for change.

At JHU, a sense of urgency around work–life issues was established early on by WORKlife Programs through a daylong work and family leadership conference held to further the goals of leadership awareness, adherence to organizational change and intervention, and the importance of the systems and life span developmental theories that support work–life programs. The leadership conference focused on work and family issues in academia and specifically at JHU. Experts on human resources, family medical leave, flexibility, and other issues spoke to more than 100 key university leaders, including the president and the Council of Deans. The day ended with leadership focus groups working on developing recommendations in four areas—benefits, dependent care, faculty and staff relationships, and work structure—that would help the university develop a more "family friendly and supportive environment." This first leadership conference brought to the fore the issues of work–life that JHI was facing, promoting a sense of urgency among campus leaders who would be specifically responsible for supporting changes to create a more family-friendly campus.

Step 2: Form a Powerful Guiding Coalition

Creating a powerful coalition committed to the vision and to the change efforts is a hallmark of the work–life organizational work over the years. This organizational work could not have been accomplished alone. The program staff always has worked broadly across JHI in groups, teams, committees, and task forces to organize and implement even the simplest service programs. These collegial structures are commonly used in academic work environments to address issues, manage business, and stimulate thinking. The importance of these working relationships cannot be ignored and must be personally maintained over time.

To create a coalition, JHU created the university-wide Work and Family Task Force (WFTF), sponsored by the vice president of human resources in

1996, and included faculty and staff from all major divisions and schools of the university. Again, WORKlife Programs provided staff support and work–life subject matter expertise. WFTF met regularly over 13 months and focused on the four major areas defined at the Work and Family Leadership Conference: benefits, dependent care, faculty and staff relationships, and work structure. By bringing people together under a university-sponsored task force, an immediate group of educated supporters was created to push forward work–life initiatives.

Evidence of the effectiveness of the coalition is found in the establishment of a report that outlined 16 recommendations that reflected a work and family perspective but are far-reaching, and as the WFTF chairs noted, "in some cases advocate significant changes to the way the University does business." The goal throughout was the "enhancement and continued development of a family-friendly environment throughout the University" (WORKlife Programs, 1997). Within a year after WFTF completed its work, Hopkins, acting on the recommendations of WFTF and the benefits committee, offered domestic partnership benefits to employees. At the same time, the division of arts and sciences and other academic divisions within the university began to wrestle with issues related to work and family and to develop policies to guide faculty in areas of family leave, dependent care, academic careers and tenure, and others.

Step 3: Create a Vision

Because the WORKlife, Employee Assistance, and Student Assistance programs were integrated under the Office of Human Services, the individuals interested in enhancing work-life balance at JHI were able to paint a compelling picture of the realities of work and family life at Hopkins. Developing data collection systems early for all three programs enabled the group to support this vision with data, making the images more powerful. Kotter supports and encourages exposure to new ideas outside the normal work of the organization, and creation of the vision was expanded by benchmarking with other institutions, providing ongoing and vital exposure to corporations performing similar work in professional associations and roundtables, and paying careful attention to national policy development and debates (e.g., family and medical leave). To create a vision, campuses need to have stakeholders discuss the national trends, explore new ideas, and articulate the vision to disseminate to the campus. JHU articulated its vision through the Work and Family Task Force.

In order to create a campuswide vision, JHU took the 16 recommendations of WFTF and prioritized them in a 5-year strategic plan. Not only did the 5-year plan articulate the vision for the campus around work–life issues, it also provided WORKlife Programs with a blueprint and an operating plan developed in partnership with university leaders, who had participated in a carefully planned and guided process that led to greater understanding and knowledge about the demands of work and personal life as social and systemic issues. Progress reports were submitted annually to the vice president of human resources and to the WFTF co-chairs, who oversaw implementation of the recommendations, and WORKlife Programs was asked to prepare a report on flexible work (Beauchesne, 1997).

Step 4: Communicate the Vision

Every vehicle possible was used to communicate the vision, including Web sites, campus newspapers, program brochures, posters, pamphlets, information fairs, workshops, and seminars. After WFTF completed its work, WORKlife Programs sought to develop new JHI constituent groups, such as the FASAP WORKlife Advisory Committee and its subcommittee, the Flexibility Work Group. These efforts provided opportunities for leaders to learn and think broadly about work–life theory, research, strategy, policies, procedures, and services and the needs of JHI. The relationships developed during ongoing meetings with key leaders promoted open discussion and exchange of issues.

To communicate the vision, administrators at JHU developed a flexible work policy for staff and placed it in the *Human Resources Policy Manual.* Based on the *Report on Flexible Work* prepared by WORKlife Programs, flexibility guidelines, procedures, and forms were developed and placed on the WORKlife Programs Web site (http://hrnt.jhu.edu/worklife/). In her memorandum to human resources staff across the university, the vice president of human resources said

> I ask you to join me in taking a leadership role in introducing flexible work arrangements to directors, managers, and supervisors in departments for which you have responsibility. As we move forward, we will learn. Sharing our experiences will help us all grow and become more comfortable with flexible ways to do the job.

Inherent in this message was the importance of working as a team and developing strategies to achieve flexible ways to work. This communication from the vice president also outlined new expected behaviors: learning and sharing experiences to produce growth, development, and organizational change. A workshop on flexibility and supportiveness at work soon followed for supervisors and managers developed and taught by WORKlife Programs. In addition, an e-training module for supervisors and staff on flexibility was placed online on the WORKlife Web site.

Step 5: Empower Others to Act on the Vision

Another important step in creating organizational change is to empower organizational constituents to take the vision and create new policies and programs. Without others feeling empowered to operationalize the vision, it remains an abstraction and will not be integrated into the culture (Kotter, 1995). At JHI, several groups across campus were empowered through workshops. For example, the Hopkins 24/7 workshops on flexibility and support for supervisors and managers were designed to promote creative thinking and nontraditional ideas, activities, and actions. The service programs in OHS assisted work–life in all areas. In addition, the Career Management Program collaborated with WORKlife Programs to develop workshops and presentations on career choice and how it relates to work and personal life, retirement planning and resources, and life span career planning. Organizational development and diversity supported the committee throughout the retreat through the expert organizational design, facilitation by its director, and development of an online questionnaire and analysis. The Center for Training and Education offered workshops, provided space, and handled enrollment and publicity. Finally, the Provost's Committee on the Status of Women invited work–life input on an ongoing basis (Beauchesne, Heiser, Jones, & Kilburg, 2004), and in its final report gave the work–life leadership development course, which was developed and piloted in 2004, a major boost with a recommendation that it should be essential learning for leaders.

After WFTF completed its work, the WORKlife Programs, FASAP, and OHS directors engaged in a series of discussions about the changing demographic, social, cultural, political, and economic stresses and strains facing faculty and staff, who were trying to work and care for their families. The aging workforce, labor shortages, and increasing health care costs now presented JHI with new human resources concerns. Furthermore, the FASAP/

WORKlife Advisory Committee (FWAC) was designed as a small think tank to provide its members with an opportunity to discuss and review trends affecting the Hopkins workforce. Members of the FWAC participated over 2½ years in discussions about organizational responses to the challenges of integrating work and personal lives. They reviewed and discussed workplace characteristics, human resources policies, organizational initiatives, work redesign, and theoretical frameworks and thought about how workers at Hopkins organize their lives and work to meet competing demands and responsibilities as adults and employees.

Step 6: Plan For and Create Short-Term Wins

When individuals are empowered and the vision is put into action, motivation will need to be sustained. Kotter (1995) suggests setting short-term goals (within the framework of long-term goals) and celebrating when those short-term goals are achieved. This highlights the success of the change effort within the organization and recognizes individuals for their efforts. At JHI, each year gains were made and recommendations were completed with visible changes in the services and in the approach of the institution. The WFTF chairs and the vice president of human resources provided oversight that ensured that the recommended changes would endure.

Step 7: Consolidate Improvements and Produce More Change

Kotter (1995) believes it takes years to guide and accomplish such organizational change. The leadership of FASAP, WORKlife Programs, and OHS was stable and continued for 20 years. The model and conceptual framework were highly used and well respected at all levels of the university and personally supported for more than 20 years by the senior university leadership team.

To achieve the long-term change mentioned earlier, attention must be paid to each step in the consolidation process. It was nearly 6 years from the end of the WFTF meetings to the development of the advisory committee leadership group. During that time, numerous work–life service programs were developed, policies and procedures changed, and support groups, workshops, and presentations organized and publicized. The program also received a number of awards and other recognition for its work. Each of these reinvigorated the staff and created institutional recognition and support. For example, early in the development of WORKlife Programs, a matrix of work–life programs was constructed using a model developed by Friedman and Galinsky (1991). The matrix was widely disseminated and included financial, counseling, educational, and benefits programs at JHI that support employees and their families across their life spans. Thus, the idea of work–life was expanded from only a couple of childcare and elder care programs to programs such as career planning and management, English as a second language, JHU credit union accounts for employee children, health screenings, a tuition grant program for college-bound children of employees, and bereavement leave. The expanded matrix showed that Hopkins already had a constellation of programs that were family friendly and emphasized life span development. The work–life matrix illustrated that these supportive services were available to all employees—not just employees with problems.

Step 8: Institutionalize New Approaches

The final stage in creating organizational change, according to Kotter (1995), is to institutionalize those new approaches or to integrate the new programs and policies into the normal operations and culture of the institution. Institutionalization was achieved at JHI by establishing new integrated offices that reflected the changing nature of work–life issues. In 2007, the new Talent Management and Organizational Development team replaced OHS. Three of the service programs (Career Management, Center for Training and Education, and Organizational Development and Diversity) were subsumed under this new structure. FASAP, the Office of WORKlife Programs, and SAP remain integrated and report directly to the vice president of human resources. The historical documents and reports have been reviewed, and recommendations for next steps are being developed.

Lessons Learned: Promoting Organizational Change Through the Office of WORKlife Programs

The achievement of excellence at work is a keystone supporting the values of the institution. For the past 16 years, the hospital has received the Best Hospital Award from *U.S. News & World Report,* and the institution's pride in this award is apparent because the posters awarded each year are immediately visible on entering the doors of the hospital. Throughout the years, the

Office of WORKlife Programs has developed programs to support employees and has won awards, and its staff has served as leaders and subject-matter experts on work–life strategy, policies, and programs (Beauchesne, 2005, 2007). Organizations that are just starting up such programs or individuals who are working in work–life programs in academia may find it useful to understand the basic strategies that were used to expand the breadth and influence of the program in important ways.

First, organizational change does not happen in a vacuum, and work–life programs in universities cannot advance the quality-of-life agenda without careful scholarship, evidence-based research, knowledge of work–life theory, and incorporating the work–life schema with other groups. Too often, work–life programs are viewed as a set of services that can be bought and housed under human resources staff coordinating positions in the organization. Each year, some colleges and universities outsource their programs. However, most recently, there is evidence that these programs may be more highly placed in colleges and universities. For example, Columbia University has demonstrated that work–life programs can be positioned at high levels in academia, because the director of work–life programs is an associate provost.

Second, it is absolutely essential to know the literature and to read widely in the field. Work–life professionals come from a variety of professional backgrounds, but there is a shared base of literature that should be at the fingertips of all in this field. Family sociology, workplace social policy, organizational development, social responsibility and corporate citizenship, and leadership are just a few of the essential subjects for those interested in developing vital and viable work–life programs in academia. In an academic environment, it is important to develop research-based frameworks that support the work–life agenda. The early work of Galinsky (1986; Galinsky, Friedman, & Hernandez, 1991a, 1991b), Friedman (Friedman et al., 1996), Bailyn (Bailyn, Drago, & Kochan, 2002), Rapoport (Rapoport & Bailyn, 1996; Rapoport, Bailyn, Fletcher, & Pruitt, 2002; Rapoport & Rapoport, 1965), and Kanter (1977) on positioning work–life programs within organizations serve as timeless and timely guides to this day. Exposure to ideas outside academia also provides fuel for new ideas and strategies. Much can be learned from corporations, many of which traveled through this work–life social and economic terrain long before colleges and universities. Careful attention to social policy in the workplace and the national debates about those policies (e.g., Family and Medical Leave Act) provide a broader understanding of the issues and ways to frame the debates.

Within FASAP, SAP, and WORKlife Programs, investing in staff education has been absolutely critical to success. The integrated framework developed early on encouraged broader thinking among program staff. Some staff worked in both programs as service providers, and all staff were required to fully understand the services of each program. Investments were made in training all program staff in both work-life and employee assistance, and all staff attended workshops on work-life and employee assistance topics. Herlihy (1996) speaks of the "turf issues" that can arise between work–life programs and EAPs because the roles and responsibilities of the two programs often are similar. WORKlife Programs has found that the integrated model generally has prevented conflicts between programs.

Last, data collection systems that enable programs to collect data for evaluation purposes and also to provide information for leadership are essential. Careful attention to data collection systems in the early years of FASAP and WORKlife Programs development enabled annual reports to be provided to leaders. Plus, the data provided to WFTF and the advisory committee were essential in creating a solid rationale and a sense of urgency. Both programs have collected more than 22 years of program and assessment data from the faculty and staff who used the programs. These data have provided a powerful and compelling glimpse into the work and personal lives of our employees and their family members. Even when the data are aggregated and anonymized, the story they tell cannot be ignored.

Conclusion

Although work–life programs have become more popular in colleges and universities over the past decade, the Johns Hopkins Institutions serves as an example of one of the forerunners in the field. Work–life and other academic staff have worked tirelessly over the past several decades to respond to the changing needs of faculty and staff by implementing an array of programs and policies. Although every college and university brings unique issues and needs, the experiences of those at JHI—with an emphasis on collaboration and seeking consensus across departments—serve as a helpful model for all interested in implementing change on their campuses.

References

Attridge, M. (2005) The business case for the integration of employee assistance, work-life, and wellness services: A literature review. In M. Attridge, P. A. Herlihy, & R. P. Maiden (Eds.), *The integration of employee assistance, work/life, and wellness services* (pp. 31–56). Binghamton, NY: Haworth Press.

Attridge, M., & Gornick, M. E. (2003). *Making the business case for EAPs and work/life: A research review and workshop.* Paper presented at the EAPA National Conference, New Orleans, LA.

Bailyn, L., Drago, R., & Kochan, T. (2002). *Integrating work and family life: A holistic approach.* Boston: Sloan Work-Family Policy Network.

Beauchesne, K. (1997). *Individualized flexible schedules: A proposal.* Report presented to the Human Resources Strategies and Implementation Committee, Baltimore, MD.

Beauchesne, K. (2005). *Hopkins 24/7: A white paper on excellence in the quality of work and personal life.* Unpublished manuscript, Johns Hopkins University.

Beauchesne, K. (2007). *The future of work: A white paper on flexible work practices in education, healthcare and research at the Johns Hopkins Institutions.* Unpublished manuscript, Johns Hopkins University.

Beauchesne, K., Heiser, L., Jones, L. D., & Kilburg, R. (2004). *Perspectives on gender-related obstacles for women faculty and staff.* Report to the University Committee on the Status of Women. Baltimore: Johns Hopkins University, Office of Human Services.

Beidel, B. (2005). An integrated EAP—defining one's place in the organization: A perspective from the internal EAP side of the fence. In M. Attridge, P. A. Herlihy, & R. P. Maiden (Eds.), *The integration of employee assistance, work/life, and wellness services* (pp. 281–306). Binghamton, NY: Haworth Press.

Bidgood, R., Boudewyn, A., & Fasbinder, B. (2005). Wells Fargo's employee assistance consulting model: How to be an invited guest at every table. In M. Attridge, P. A. Herlihy, & R. P. Maiden (Eds.), *The integration of employee assistance, work/life, and wellness services* (pp. 219–242). Binghamton, NY: Haworth Press.

Friedman, D. E. (1991). *Linking work and family issues to the bottom line.* New York: Conference Board.

Friedman, D., & Galinsky, E. (1991). *The FWI family-friendly index: A self-assessment guide for corporations.* New York: Families & Work Institute.

Friedman, D., & Johnson, A. (1991). *Moving from programs to culture change: The next state for the corporate work-family agenda.* New York: Families & Work Institute.

Friedman, D. E., Rimsky, C., & Johnson, A. A. (1996). *College and university reference guide to work-family programs: Report on a collaborative study.* New York: Families & Work Institute.

Galinsky, E. (1986). Family life and corporate policies. In M. Yogman & T. B. Brazelton (Eds.), *In support of families* (pp. 109–145). Boston: Harvard University Press.

Galinsky, E., Friedman, D., & Hernandez, C. A. (1991a). *The corporate reference guide to work-family programs.* New York: Families & Work Institute.

Galinsky, E., Friedman, D. E., & Hernandez, C. A. (1991b). *Work-family programs.* New York: Families & Work Institute.

Ginsberg, M. R., Kilburg, R. R., and Gomes, P. G. (1994, August). Integrated human services and EAPs: The Johns Hopkins experience. *EAPA Exchange,* 8–10.

Ginsberg, M. R., Kilburg, R. R., & Gomes, P. G. (1999). Organizational counseling and the delivery of integrated human services in the workplace: An evolving model for employee assistance theory and practice. In J. H. Oher (Ed.), *The employee assistance handbook* (pp. 439–456). New York: Wiley.

Gornick, M. E., & Blair, B. (2005). Employee assistance, work-life effectiveness, and health and productivity: A conceptual framework for integration. In M. Attridge, P. A. Herlihy, & R. P. Maiden (Eds.), *The integration of employee assistance, work/life, and wellness services* (pp. 1–30). Binghamton, NY: Haworth Press.

Herlihy, P. (1996). *Examination of integration of EAP and work/family programs in corporations.* Unpublished doctoral dissertation, Brandeis University.

Herlihy, P. A., & Attridge, M. (2005). Research on the integration of employee assistance, work-life, and wellness services: Past, present, and future. In M. Attridge, P. A. Herlihy, & R. P. Maiden (Eds.), *The integration of employee assistance, work/life, and wellness services* (pp. 67–94). Binghamton, NY: Haworth Press.

Kanter, R. M. (1977). *Work and family in the United States: A critical review and policy agenda.* New York: Russell Sage Foundation.

Kotter, J. P. (1995). Leading change: Why transformation efforts fail. Harvard Business Review. Reprint R0701. Retrieved April 15, 2008, from http://www.hbrreprints.org

Rapoport, R., & Bailyn, L. (1996). *Relinking life and work: Toward a better future. A report to the Ford Foundation.* New York: Ford Foundation.

Rapoport, R., Bailyn, L., Fletcher, J. K., & Pruitt, B. H. (2002). *Beyond work-family balance: Advancing gender equity and workplace performance.* San Francisco: Jossey-Bass.

Rapoport, R. N., & Rapoport, R. (1965). Work and family in contemporary society. *American Sociological Review, 30,* 381–394.

Thompson, D. A., & Swihart, D. L. (2005). University of Arizona Life & Work Connections: A synergistic strategy for maximizing whole-person productivity over the employees' life-cycle/work cycle. In M. Attridge, P. A. Herlihy, & R. P. Maiden (Eds.), *The integration of employee assistance, work/life, and wellness services* (pp. 105–121). Binghamton, NY: Haworth Press.

Turner, S., Weiner, M., & Keegan, K. (2005). Ernst & Young's Assist: How internal and external service integration created a single source solution. In M. Attridge, P. A. Herlihy, & R. P. Maiden (Eds.), *The integration of employee assistance, work/life, and wellness services* (pp. 243–262). Binghamton, NY: Haworth Press.

WORKlife Programs. (1997). *The Johns Hopkins University work and family task force report.* Baltimore: Johns Hopkins University. Retrieved December 12, 2008, from http://hrnt.jhu.edu/worklife/taskforce/report.cfm

6

THE DEVIL IS IN THE DETAILS

Creating Family-Friendly Departments for Faculty at the University of California

Karie Frasch, Angelica Stacy, Mary Ann Mason,
Sharon Page-Medrich, and Marc Goulden

All the rules and policies in the world cannot help faculty and their families if administrators are not kind and supportive people. One administrator (who was my chair, and then associate dean when my child was little) was truly supportive to me, and facilitated my life as a mother and a scholar. I am extremely grateful to her. She is someone who has made a huge difference to my life and to that of my family. She established and helped maintain my commitment to the University of California.

—Female faculty member (Mason, Stacy, & Goulden, 2003, *The UC Faculty Work and Family Survey.* Unless noted, all quotes are drawn from this source.)

The University of California's ability to attract and retain the best faculty over the next decade will depend largely on having a culture that values and supports both the work and family life needs of all faculty over the course of their careers. Because the tenure clock generally overlaps with the biological clock, female faculty often face particular challenges in achieving balance and success. Moving beyond the establishment of university-wide family accommodation policies, this chapter focuses on the devil-in-the-details nature of creating cultural change within individual departments, because this is the level at which most faculty experience daily work life (Frasch, Mason, Stacy, Goulden, & Hoffman, 2007). Within this context, department chairs and deans have a central responsibility in understanding the importance of a family-friendly department and in implementing overall university policies, sharing resources, and reinforcing cultural practices to assist all faculty (Quinn, 2007; Riskin, Yen, & Quinn, 2006).

The Evolution of Family Accommodation Policies at the University of California

In 2006, the University of California (UC) made significant improvements to a comprehensive package of flexible family-friendly policies for ladder-rank faculty with caregiving responsibilities. This historic effort was the result of a 3-year period of internal examination, including discussions by administrators and faculty throughout the UC system. Before these enhancements, in 1988, UC was one of the first academic institutions to put in place formal family accommodations and was considered a leader in its commitment to the success of its faculty. However, following the release of findings from the 2003 *UC Faculty Work and Family Survey* of more than 4,400 tenure-track and tenured faculty respondents across the UC system, it became clear that the existing policies could be improved, and that creating policies alone does not change the culture toward acceptance of career flexibility (Mason, Stacy, Goulden, Hoffman, & Frasch, 2005).

Although UC's initial family-friendly accommodation policies had been in place for more than 15 years, many faculty were unaware of their existence. Only about a quarter of respondents knew about all four major policies—active service modified duties (ASMD), tenure clock extension, paid maternity leave, and unpaid parental leave (see Figure 6.1). A male faculty member commented, "Departments are the principal unit for most faculty here, but on the whole departments are inadequately staffed to update and educate faculty. As it is, much of the information is passed on by way of an 'oral tradition.' It works if you are in the loop, and tends to benefit those faculty (especially those with tenure) who have been around longer."

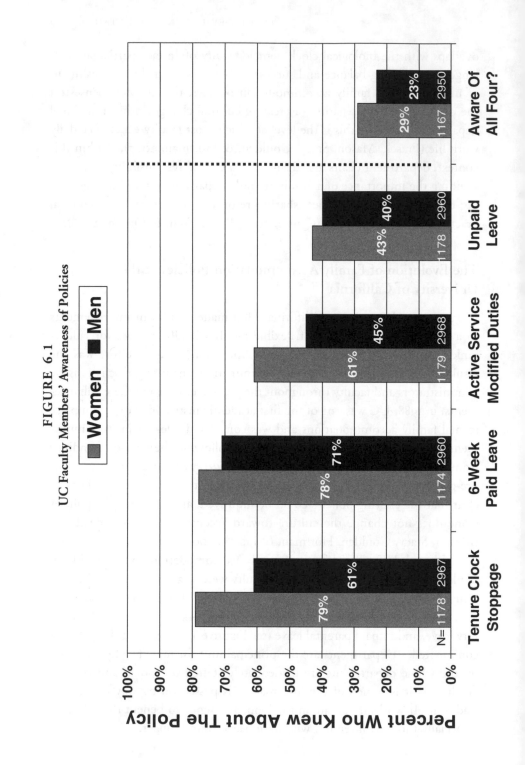

FIGURE 6.1
UC Faculty Members' Awareness of Policies

Of those faculty who were eligible to use the policies at one point in their career, many chose not to do so (see Figure 6.2), often because they feared negative career repercussions; more than half of eligible women who chose not to take ASMD said that they did not use the policy because they feared it would hurt their chances for tenure or promotion. A female faculty member said, "All of the maternity benefits were lumped under the same heading by the chair as 'unfair advantage.' I saw the two other women with young children get punished on reviews for not getting enough published even though they 'had time off and had more time to write.' I wasn't going to risk it." This fear-based response is observable not only in the low use rates of existing family-friendly policies by eligible faculty, but also in the conscious efforts of faculty women to delay or forgo fertility. Delaying child rearing is often not the desire of female faculty—40% of our faculty women (compared to just 20% of men) past the age of likely fertility (ages 40 to 60) indicated that they had fewer children than they wanted.

Following from these findings, the University of California made significant changes to its family accommodation policies. Among the most fundamental is the now unambiguous message that faculty men and women with substantial caregiving responsibilities, or those who give birth to or adopt a child, are *entitled* to the use of the appropriate family accommodation policies (rather than *may request* them); the cost of replacement teachers is centralized at the university level to eliminate hardship for individual departments. Also explicitly stated in the *Academic Personnel Manual* is a directive that peer reviewers may not act with prejudice in their evaluation of the promotions or advancement of faculty who use the policies (University of California, 2006).

The UC family accommodations package is designed to support faculty over their life course. Birth mothers receive fully paid childbearing leave. New parents, birth or adoptive, with substantial caregiving responsibilities (50% or more of care) are entitled to a full term of active service modified duties (ASMD), typically teaching relief; biological mothers receive a second term. Assistant professors who are new parents with substantial caregiving responsibilities can extend the tenure clock for one year per birth or adoption (for a maximum of 2 years during the probationary period). All parents may at any time request up to a year of unpaid parental leave. The chancellor has the authority to approve sick leave for faculty to care for themselves or their family members for an unspecified period of time. Faculty with family needs

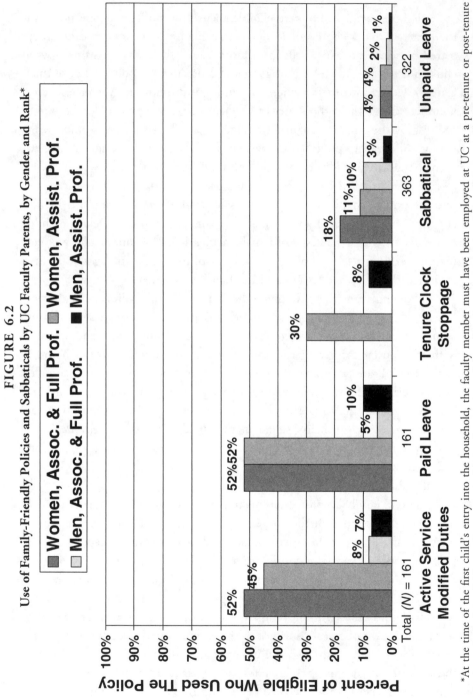

FIGURE 6.2

Use of Family-Friendly Policies and Sabbaticals by UC Faculty Parents, by Gender and Rank*

*At the time of the first child's entry into the household, the faculty member must have been employed at UC at a pre-tenure or post-tenure faculty rank, and the child must have arrived after implementation of the policy (August 1, 1988).

can be granted a permanent change or temporary reduction in the percentage of time of a full-time appointment. This comprehensive package of policies, one of the most progressive in the country, goes a long way toward creating an environment where caregivers can succeed in their academic careers while also having a satisfying family life. The experiences of individual faculty, however, depend to a great extent on the culture of the department they work in, including the attitudes of department chairs and other faculty (Drago et al., 2005).

Creating a Family-Friendly Department

Findings from the *UC Faculty Work and Family Survey* clearly indicate that changing the culture of the university requires not only robust policies but also practical solutions for women and men balancing work and family. Improvements to family accommodation policies on the books can help alleviate some of the challenges, but appropriate assessment and implementation is central to making the policies meaningful. As the front-line administrators for each department, chairs and deans have a unique obligation to be leaders in the effort to promote family friendliness (Riskin et al., 2006).

Based on our experiences at the University of California as well as empirical findings from many sources, this section offers guidance for department chairs, or others advocating for change, to follow. Change includes three major phases: assessment, implementation, and devil-is-in-the-details. Although this process could be undertaken at any time, it is most likely to succeed if a baseline of family accommodation policies are already in place at the institution (please refer to other chapters in this book for advice and strategies for creating or improving family-friendly policies).

Phase 1: Assessment

The first phase of cultural transformation involves four steps (not necessarily in this order): knowing the importance of making family friendliness a priority, evaluating the department's current practices and climate, understanding cultural and unconscious bias issues, and knowing the potential legal ramifications if policies are not supported.

Step 1: Make understanding the importance of family friendliness a major priority and goal for your department. Failure to understand the importance of family friendliness, particularly in the sciences, results in fewer women and a less diverse faculty overall (Mason, Goulden, & Frasch, n.d.). All department chairs and deans, as well as faculty, should be familiar with the overwhelming data on the negative effects of the academic structure on the academic pipeline for women. (See published reports and papers, such as American Council on Education, 2005; Committee on Maximizing the Potential of Women in Academic Science and Engineering, 2006). At Berkeley we've observed that, compared to the pool of qualified Ph.D. candidates, women underapply to faculty positions relative to their national rates of academic achievement (Mason et al., 2005). Detailed analyses from the Survey of Doctorate Recipients (SDR)—a biennial weighted, longitudinal study following more than 160,000 Ph.D. recipients across all disciplines until they reach age 76—help explain these issues, which can be accounted for, in part, by differential dynamics of family formation. For each year after the Ph.D., married men with children under age 6 are 50% more likely to enter a tenure-track position than are married women with children under age 6. Single women without children (or those who have them more than 5 years after the Ph.D.) do as well as married men with young children. Overall, for each year after securing a tenure-track position, men are 20% more likely to achieve tenure than women (Mason & Goulden, 2002; Wolfinger, Mason, & Goulden, forthcoming).

Faculty careers often have a negative effect on women's family lives. Using the SDR, analyses of the life courses of Ph.D. recipients show that only one in three women without children who take a fast-track university job ever become mothers; women who achieve tenure are more than twice as likely as men who achieve tenure to be single 12 years out from the Ph.D.; and if married, faculty women are significantly more likely than faculty men to experience divorce or separation (Mason & Goulden, 2004). One of the reasons why women leave the academy and have such different family formation patterns from male faculty is the tension between work and family responsibilities—a tension experienced more strongly by women (Mason et al., 2005). Knowing this information is valuable for making the links between family friendliness, faculty composition, and faculty satisfaction.

Step 2: Review and assess your department's current practices and climate. Women with family caregiving needs sometimes contend with a sense of hostility from colleagues and an unwelcoming or alienating campus climate. This atmosphere is often invisible to many men, who tend to describe a better climate for women than women themselves report, as indicated by faculty surveys at UC Berkeley, MIT, Princeton, the University of Michigan, and the University of Wisconsin (Handelsman et al., 2005; UC Berkeley Office for Faculty Equity, 2004). In departments with a skewed gender distribution, typically with many more men than women, women commonly have this experience (University of Michigan ADVANCE Program, 2007). In this case, it is unlikely that women, especially more junior faculty, will readily express their opinions.

Departments can begin to assess their climate and equity issues by reviewing any available data from campuswide surveys and then examining objective information in areas such as salary, merit raises, space and equipment or other resources, administrative support, promotions, and teaching and committee assignments. To learn about the experiences of individual faculty members, department chairs can create a diverse committee to conduct interviews and meetings with all faculty and set clear ground rules for interactions. If the goal of creating a positive departmental climate is clearly communicated by the dean and department chair, female faculty are more likely to feel safe expressing unpopular or negative views. Careful listening and expressed empathy alone can go a long way toward improving the climate.

Step 3: Become conscious about unconscious bias issues concerning caregiving and gender. Numerous studies on the role of unconscious and implicit assumptions reveal that even the most careful people (both men and women) have biases related to caregiving and gender (Nosek, Banaji, & Greenwald, 2008; Williams, 2001; Women in Science and Engineering Leadership Institute [WISELI], 2005). People are often unaware of their implicit biases, even when their behavior reflects them. For example, in a study of job seekers (Correll & Benard, 2005), male and female evaluators were asked to rate a candidate randomly assigned a male or female name and parental status. When asked whether they would hire the applicant, 84% of participants said they would hire a woman without children, but only 47% would hire a mother. In assigning a pay range, nonmothers were offered $11,000 more than mothers. In contrast, fathers were offered $6,000 more in salary than nonfathers. In another study, 238 male and female academic psychologists were asked to evaluate an identical curriculum vitae randomly assigned a male or a female name. Both male and female participants were more likely to hire the male applicant and also gave the male applicant better evaluations for teaching, research, and service experience (Steinpreis, Anders, & Ritzke, 1999).

Department chairs, and all faculty, can learn about their unconscious biases by reading summaries of the wealth of research in this area. They can also initiate discussions on the topic through brown-bag lunches or workshops. Project Implicit (http://www.projectimplicit.net), an online tool and associated collection of research, provides an easy way to become conscious about these issues through self-assessments. Research indicates that evaluators who are busy, distracted by other tasks, or experiencing stress are more likely to engage in evaluations that are based on assumptions (WISELI, 2005), so providing sufficient time and resources is critical. When hiring and promotion committees are aware of implicit biases, they can work to minimize their influence on evaluations. Similarly, chairs and others can consider the ways in which their assumptions may or may not contribute to a less positive climate for women and all caregivers.

Step 4: Be aware of and understand the variety of legal issues related to the role of department chair, including the fact that failure to support policies and laws can, in extreme cases, result in litigation. Unfortunately, in some instances before 2006, UC faculty who requested the use of family accommodations encountered resistance from their department chair; memories of these types of experiences percolate through the culture of the university and undermine a collective sense of family friendliness. Examples of negative responses to past requests for family accommodations at UC include the following: "I want to emphasize that the greatest source of work-related stress in relation to having a child has been the hostility and recalcitrance of my chair who announced that he thought of ASMD as a 'special privilege' and who fought it all the way" (female faculty member); "I received a sneering denial by my chair, who said that, while another male colleague at [UC] may have enjoyed that 'vacation' our department couldn't spare my teaching services" (male faculty member referring to denial of ASMD by chair); "I was told by my department chair, as untenured faculty, actually using the stopped tenure clock or leave would be held against me. I was back teaching a day after getting out of the hospital" (female faculty member); and "My chairman initially tried to pressure me to not take ASMD 'for the good of the department' because he did not want to set a precedent and because he said that the university would not reimburse the department for the expense of hiring a replacement teacher" (male faculty member).

Most department chairs do not receive training on legal issues related to family accommodations. Having a working knowledge of the main policies that affect faculty is necessary because if conflicts arise, the principles of the university will be used as the basis of judgment (Connel, Franke, & Lee, 2001; Hecht, Higgerson, Gmelch, & Tucker, 1999). Comments made by administrators have been offered as evidence in litigation over the denial of tenure from various institutions (Euben, 2004; Franke & White, 2000; Williams, 2004), and women have won recent court cases. A 2005 ruling by the federal Equal Employment Opportunity Commission (EEOC) found "reasonable cause" that a female assistant professor was a victim of sex discrimination when she was turned down for tenure. The professor's complaint, supported by the EEOC, stated that her department gave her work rave reviews until she took two leaves, one each for the birth of her two daughters. After that time, other faculty members raised doubts about how productive she would be and ultimately denied her tenure despite an impressive teaching and publication record and positive assessment from experts in her field. She was subsequently granted retroactive tenure (Jaschik, 2005).

Choosing to do a thorough assessment of the department culture and to prioritize becoming family friendly is a major commitment; results will not occur overnight. Evaluating the current environment may turn up issues and concerns that do not have easy answers as well as resistance from some faculty, particularly senior faculty who may be more invested in maintaining the status quo. However, the long-term payoff for making the culture of every department welcoming and supportive of those with caregiving needs will far exceed the up-front investment.

Phase 2: Implementation

The second phase, implementation, includes learning what the family accommodation policies and applicable laws are that apply to different faculty constituents, actively highlighting them, being proactive about recruiting faculty with diverse experiences and backgrounds, and advocating for faculty during the promotion and tenure process.

Step 1: Know the family accommodation policies and laws that apply to your faculty. Department chairs are charged with an enormous range of tasks and responsibilities. Most serve in the role for only a few years, and many receive little training. Family accommodation policies and laws are just a few of the hundreds of policies they are expected to know about. Unfortunately, most faculty turn to their department chair to learn about applicable policies and expect them to be knowledgeable. When department chairs give incorrect information, it is usually faculty members who suffer. Universities can help department chairs by creating toolkits with summarized information on a variety of topics as well as Web links to complete information. Department chair leadership workshops are also invaluable. At the University of California, we have a toolkit specifically on family-friendly issues called *Creating a Family Friendly Department: Chairs and Deans Toolkit* (Frasch et al., 2007). Whether or not a toolkit exists, department chairs are responsible for knowing what the policies are and how they are applied to individual situations.

Step 2: Actively highlight, advertise, and support your department's family accommodation policies and procedures, benefits, and resources for all faculty (including recruits). Taking this step involves having and sharing a vision of what the department should be like and helps assure faculty that they will not be arbitrarily disadvantaged in promotion, advancement, or compensation. Communicating this information regularly and consistently through e-mail, written correspondence, departmental meetings, and newsletters helps everyone know that the department is committed to being family friendly. Solicit, gather, and disseminate family-friendly materials and brochures for this purpose.

Junior faculty, particularly women, can also benefit greatly from mentoring by department chairs or senior faculty about combining work and family. To counter feelings that work–family balance is a unique situation to be figured out alone, junior faculty need to hear from and see others who successfully balance their professional and personal lives without negative repercussions. For example, UC Davis's Faculty Advisors for Work Life program (http://academicpersonnel.ucdavis.edu/worklife/default.cfm) has a group of trained senior faculty from a variety of departments who are available to consult and share wisdom and experiences of balancing work and family in academia. Faculty can seek them out and speak confidentially about concerns or issues. The advisors also publicize and provide information to the campus on family-friendly policies and programs.

Step 3: Be proactive about recruiting and hiring diverse faculty for your department, including those who have temporarily slowed down their career for family caregiving reasons. Communicate that your department is a place where faculty with current or potential caregiving responsibilities will thrive (University of Michigan ADVANCE Program, 2007; University of Washington ADVANCE Center for Institutional Change, 2006). For scholars who delay their academic careers to start families or provide care to others, it is extremely difficult to return to academia by securing tenure-track or postdoctoral positions. Faculty hiring committees often view these applicants as suspect because of gaps in their vitae and the time that has elapsed since they received their Ph.D.s. Departments can set a positive example for others and help combat the loss of potentially excellent scholars by encouraging faculty hiring committees to discount caregiving-related résumé gaps.

When recruiting finalists, department chairs or hiring committees should provide or make use of dual-career assistance, relocation assistance, and childcare support. In a 2006–2007 UC Berkeley survey of departmental hiring practices (Stacy & Goulden, 2006), department chairs rated the impact of 18 recruitment factors in their effect on the successful recruitment of first-choice candidates. The three factors with the most negative reported impact on recruitment were all related to relocation: the availability of housing, good schools, and high-quality childcare. These issues are more likely to affect female candidates.

Lack of support for dual-career issues may result in losing some of the best talent. Approximately 80% of academics have partners who are employed professionally (Didion, 1996); female academics are more likely to be affected by dual-career concerns because of their higher rate of marriage to other academics (approximately 40%); and women employed in the sciences are particularly likely to be partnered with other scientists (Astin & Milem, 1997; McNeil & Sher, 1998). Overall, women are more likely to defer to a male partner's career—either by leaving the academic pipeline or by not considering moving because of partner or family concerns.

Step 4: Establish and maintain transparency in the promotion and tenure process. Department chairs need to be advocates for faculty who have used family accommodation policies through the promotion and tenure process. The more information faculty who have used the policies are given about their progress toward advancement or tenure, the more likely it is that they will view the environment as open and the chair as someone they can trust (University of Washington ADVANCE Center for Institutional Change, 2007). One faculty member said, "When I was chair of the campus Committee on Appointments and Promotions, I had to 'remind' male colleagues on the committee regularly that 'stop the clock' time does not count in the calculation of years at UC!" Deans, budget committees, and outside reviewers should be directed to focus on quality and total quantity of scholarly productivity, rather than time since degree or job hire, so that faculty who slow down because of family obligations are not unduly penalized in the peer review process. This information can be conveyed through standardized forms or sample letters at the level of central administration or directly from the department.

These steps, implemented together, link the knowledge acquired through assessing the state of the department with respect to these issues with actions to support current and future faculty through all phases of their academic career. However, additional steps are needed to ensure that the culture becomes one that enables all faculty to have both a successful work and family life.

Phase 3: Devil-Is-in-the-Details

The overall success of cultural transformation depends on considering and including the details, the seemingly more minor practices or programs that contribute to the larger goal. Not doing so can derail any amount of good intention.

Step 1: Make the use of family accommodations the standard for conducting business in your department rather than viewing them as exceptions or "special privileges." When departments can access centralized funding to cover the replacement costs of teachers for faculty who take leave, it is much easier to make the use of family accommodation policies standard practice because the burden on the department is much less. However, even when this is not the case, department chairs need to adopt and convey the attitude that most faculty, both men and women, will want to use the family accommodation policies for which they are eligible. Supporting faculty in using the policies is an investment in the future success of individuals as well as the health of the department. One faculty member aptly said, "Department chairs should encourage, not discourage, faculty from using them. Their use should become a regular part of the personnel system, not the exception. Information about how many faculty use the policies should be published to encourage their use."

Step 2: Maintain zero tolerance for discriminatory and disparaging comments and behaviors. Make clear to all faculty that hostile comments and behaviors are unacceptable and violate the rules governing professional conduct (for example, see the University of California *Academic Personnel Manual,* APM-015, The Faculty Code of Conduct, http://www.ucop.edu/acadadv/acadpers/apm/apm-015.pdf). Be a model for the department by treating all faculty with dignity and respect, both in public settings and in face-to-face situations. If a faculty member indicates that negative comments have been made, take immediate action to learn more about the situation and resolve whatever issues come to the fore. Conversely, regularly and publicly acknowledge efforts made by faculty or administrators to improve the departmental climate.

Step 3: Implement small changes that can have a significant impact on the culture of your department. When approached by faculty members needing to use family accommodation policies, encourage them to use the policies in whatever way works best for them and their family, rather than what may be most convenient for the department. During pregnancy, some women may benefit from or need modifications to their position, for example, transferring to a less strenuous or hazardous position if it is medically necessary and can be reasonably accommodated. Also, work closely with faculty members to determine course and committee assignments that may be more manageable during the semester of their return from a leave.

The scheduling of faculty meetings, classes, seminars, and receptions should take into account the competing and often simultaneous demands of work and caregiving for faculty trying to excel in both realms (as one female faculty member reported, "Meetings and events very often conflict with the end of the childcare day. Guilt and failure on all fronts is a given"). Whenever possible, departmental events should be scheduled between 8 a.m. and 5 p.m. (during regular childcare provider hours). A small change of this type can have a large impact on departmental culture, feelings of inclusion among faculty, and faculty success in the academic arena.

Dispelling myths about lack of seriousness among faculty who extend the clock to meet family needs, or nursing mothers who bring babies to conferences or presentations, for example, will go far in fostering a family-friendly culture. The provision of a travel fund for faculty (particularly breast-feeding mothers) who must bring a young child with them for research or conferences, or who must hire additional help when they are away, should exist at the department or campus level.

Step 4: Periodically assess the effectiveness of your efforts toward family friendliness. After an initial assessment of department climate, set clearly defined goals and expectations for improvement. These may be a combination of objective measures (Has the number of faculty in the department who have used family accommodation policies increased? Are salaries equitable between men and women? etc.) and more subjective measures (How do different faculty constituents feel about the climate? Are there more open and direct conversations about the importance of balancing work and personal life? etc.). When initially assessing the climate of the department, communicate clearly to faculty that the goals that are set will be continually evaluated. Reassess the effectiveness of the efforts at regular intervals (e.g., yearly), and publicly announce the results to the department.

Conclusion

Through our experience on the UC Faculty Family Friendly Edge projects, we have learned that introducing policy changes is a much more straightforward process than enacting cultural transformation. But the investment in the culture of the institution is critical. No amount of well-crafted policy on the books can take the place of support and goodwill, the necessary ingredients of a family-friendly culture. This generation of upcoming young scholars is different in many ways from those of just 30 or 40 years ago—men and women fill the ranks in nearly equal numbers, and they value and expect flexibility and balance between their career and other life goals. Becoming truly family friendly is an indispensable component of success for institutions that want to attract and keep the best faculty throughout their careers.

References

American Council on Education. (2005). *An agenda for excellence: Creating flexibility in tenure-track faculty careers.* Washington, DC: Author.

Astin, H. S., & Milem, J. F. (1997). The status of academic couples in U.S. institutions. In M. A. Ferber and J. W. Loeb (Eds.), *Academic couples: Problems and promises* (pp. 128–155). Urbana: University of Illinois Press.

Committee on Maximizing the Potential of Women in Academic Science and Engineering. (2006). *Beyond bias and barriers: Fulfilling the potential of women in academic science and engineering.* Washington, DC: National Academies Press.

Connel, M. A., Franke, A. H., & Lee, B. A. (2001). Agency and indemnification. Retrieved March 31, 2008, from http://www.acenet.edu/resources/chairs/docs/Connell_agency_in demn.pdf

Correll, S. J., & Benard, S. W. (2005). *Getting a job: Is there a motherhood penalty?* Paper presented at the annual meeting of the American Sociological Association, Philadelphia, PA.

Didion, C. J. (1996). Dual careers and shared positions: Adjusting university policy to accommodate academic couples. *Journal of College Science Teaching, 26*(2), 123–124.

Drago, R., Colbeck, C., Stauffer, K. D., Pirretti, A., Burkum, K., Fazioli, J., et al. (2005). Bias against caregiving. *Academe, 91*(5), 22–25.

Euben, D. R. (2004). Legal watch: Family matters. *Academe, 90*(6), 31.

Franke, A. H., & White, L. (2000). *Responsibilities of department chairs: Legal issues.* Prepared for Collaboration Toward the Common Good: Faculty and Administration Working Together conference, Washington, DC. Retrieved March 31, 2008, from http://www.acenet.edu/resources/chairs/docs/franke_white.pdf

Frasch, K., Mason, M. A., Stacy, A., Goulden, M., & Hoffman, C. (2007). *Creating a family friendly department: Chairs and deans toolkit.* University of California, Berkeley. Retrieved April 9, 2008, from http://ucfamilyedge.berkeley.edu/toolkit.html

Handelsman, J., Cantor, N., Carnes, M., Denton, D., Fine, E., Grosz, B., et al. (2005). Careers in science: Enhanced: More women in science. *Science, 309*(5783), 1190–1191.

Hecht, I. W., Higgerson, M. L., Gmelch, W. H., & Tucker, A. (1999). Legal issues for chairs. In *The department chair as academic leader* (pp. 212–214). Phoenix, AZ: ACE Oryx Press.

Jaschik, S. (2005, September 15). Faux family friendly? *Inside Higher Ed.* Retrieved December 12, 2008, from http://www.insidehighered.com/news/2005/09/15/ucsb

Mason, M. A., & Goulden, M. (2002). Do babies matter? The effect of family formation on the lifelong careers of academic men and women. *Academe, 88*(6), 21–27.

Mason, M. A., & Goulden, M. (2004). Do babies matter (Part II)? Closing the baby gap. *Academe, 90*(6), 10–15.

Mason, M. A., Goulden, M., & Frasch, K. (n.d.). A bad reputation: Why doctoral students are rejecting the academic fast track. Manuscript submitted for publication.

Mason, M. A., Stacy, A., & Goulden, M. (2003). *The UC faculty work and family survey.* University of California, Berkeley. Retrieved April 9, 2008, from http://ucfamilyedge.berkeley.edu

Mason, M. A., Stacy, A., Goulden, M., Hoffman, C., & Frasch, K. (2005). *The UC Faculty Family Friendly Edge: An initiative for tenure-track faculty at the University of California.* Report. University of California, Berkeley. Retrieved April 9, 2008, from http:// ucfamilyedge.berkeley.edu/ucfamilyedge.pdf

McNeil, L., & Sher, M. (1998). The dual-career-couple problem. *Physics Today, 52*(7), 32–37.

Nosek, B., Banaji, M., & Greenwald, T. (2008). *Project Implicit.* Harvard University. Retrieved March 15, 2008, from http://www.projectimplicit.net/index.php

Quinn, K. (2007). Exploring departmental leadership: How department chairs can be transformative leaders. *InterActions: UCLA Journal of Education and Information Studies, 3*(1), 1–19.

Riskin, E., Yen, J., & Quinn, K. (2006). *Demystifying family-friendly policies for faculty: Resources for department chairs.* American Society for Engineering Education. Retrieved April 16, 2008, from http://staff.washington.edu/kquinn/Kate/ASEE_2006-1089.pdf

Stacy, A., & Goulden, M. (2006). *University of California, Berkeley Department Chair Survey.* Office for Faculty Equity, Associate Vice Provost for Faculty Equity.

Steinpreis, R. E., Anders, K. A., & Ritzke, D. (1999). The impact of gender on the review of the curricula vitae of job applicants and tenure candidates: A national empirical study. *Sex Roles, 41,* 509–528.

UC Berkeley Office for Faculty Equity. (2004). *Confidential climate survey for UC Berkeley ladder-rank faculty.* Retrieved March 31, 2008, from http://gradresearch.berkeley.edu/UCBclime.html

University of California (2006). *Academic Personnel Manual,* APM-760, Family Accommodations for Childbearing and Childrearing. Retrieved April 9, 2008, from www.ucop.edu/acadadv/acadpers/apm/apm-760.pdf

University of Michigan ADVANCE Program. (2007). *Handbook for faculty searches and hiring.* Retrieved March 31, 2008, from http://www.umich.edu/~advproj/handbook.pdf

University of Washington ADVANCE Center for Institutional Change. (2006). *Faculty retention toolkit.* Retrieved March 31, 2008, from http://www.engr.washington.edu/advance/resources/Retention/index.html

University of Washington ADVANCE Center for Institutional Change. (2007). *Faculty recruitment toolkit.* Retrieved March 31, 2008, from http://www.washington.edu/diversity/avpfa/Recruitment_Toolkit/index.html

Williams, J. (2001). *Unbending gender: Why family and work conflict and what to do about it.* New York: Oxford University Press.

Williams, J. (2004). Hitting the maternal wall. *Academe, 90*(6), 8–12.

Wolfinger, N. H., Mason, M. A., & Goulden, M. (forthcoming). Problems in the pipeline: Gender, marriage, and fertility in the ivory tower. *Journal of Higher Education.*

Women in Science and Engineering Leadership Institute (WISELI). (2005). Influence of unconscious assumptions and biases. In *Enhancing department climate: A chair's role.* Retrieved March 31, 2008, from http://wiseli.engr.wisc.edu/initiatives/climate/ResourceBook_05 .pdf

7

SHAPING THE WORK ENVIRONMENT AND FAMILY-FRIENDLY POLICIES

A Perspective from Deans

Sharon A. McDade and Sharon A. Dannels

I n the contest for talented faculty in a global marketplace, higher education institutions must compete with family-friendly policies or risk losing vital human capital to other universities or employment sectors
(Broad, 2005; Clark, 2004). Higher education presidents and chief academic
affairs officers are at the top of their institutions and thus the ultimate players
in the adoption of human resource policies (American Council on Education, 2005). Faculty relate to doing their work not at the institution but
rather at the school or college level (Schuster & Finkelstein, 2006).Thus,
deans are particularly well placed to have an impact relating to work climate
and family-friendly policies (Wolverton & Gmelch, 2002).

This chapter considers family-friendly policies and work climate from
one sector of higher education—academic medicine and dentistry—to find
lessons about how deans perceive and make sense of these issues. Academic
medicine and dentistry provide a window into issues of family-friendly policies and work climate because of how these sectors straddle academic and
nonacademic marketplaces (Kirch et al., 2005). Clinical medical and dental
faculties are involved in teaching and research similar to the work and expectations of faculty in the other disciplines of higher education (Bunton &

Mallon, 2007). However, the bulk of medical faculty (85%) are also clinicians who provide services through hospitals and health organizations that function within corporate medicine and business (Association of American Medical Colleges [AAMC], 2007a). To keep talented employees in highly competitive global marketplaces, medical and dental school deans should be attuned to the use of family-friendly policies in hospitals and health systems as deciding factors in where these employees choose to work (Kirch, 2008). The perceptions of deans of academic medicine and dental schools may provide insights regarding roles and responsibilities for all deans on these issues.

This chapter begins with a context of critical mass theory and demographics as a lens for understanding the impetus for the advent of family-friendly policies. After introducing a survey of deans of U.S. and Canadian medical and dental schools, the chapter provides the perspectives of these deans regarding family-friendly policies, work climate, and the connections between them. The chapter concludes with considerations derived from this study with applicability to deans across all sectors of higher education.

Context

The advancement of family-friendly policies can be understood from theoretical and demographic viewpoints within academic dentistry and medicine. The theoretical framework of critical mass (Ely, 1995; Kanter, 1977) postulates that the size of a group in an organization makes a difference in its impact. Kanter (1977) suggested that a 20% level in an organization and Ely (1995) showed that at least 15% in leadership positions were needed for a group to have impact on organizational policies, attitudes, norms, and support and to address gender stereotyping.

Women are at their highest representation in the history of U.S. higher education. Today (all numbers rounded to nearest whole number), women number 45% of doctoral graduates, 41% of all faculty, 25% of full professors, and 23% of university presidents (American Council on Education, 2007; Hoffer et al., 2006; National Center for Education Statistics, 2008). The story is different in academic medicine and dentistry, although women's numbers have been slowly growing in these fields. In U.S. academic dentistry, women are now 44% of students, 30% of full-time dental faculty, and 22% of deans (American Dental Education Association [ADEA], 2007,

2008; Executive Leadership in Academic Medicine [ELAM], 2008b). In academic medicine, women account for 49% of students, 34% of faculty, 16% of full professors, and 12% of U.S. accredited allopathic medical school deans (AAMC, 2007a, 2007b; ELAM, 2008b). Women in academic medicine and dentistry have achieved Kanter's (1977) critical mass of 15% within an organization for students and total faculty, and approach Ely's (1995) 15% benchmark for critical mass in senior leadership.

Apart from the significantly lower representation of women in academic medicine and dentistry compared to higher education as a whole, the role of academicians is similar except for greater service responsibilities as clinicians (Bunton & Mallon, 2007). Medicine and dentistry basic science faculty carry research obligations more in line with faculty at research and doctoral-granting institutions. Although clinical faculty also teach and conduct research, they have service obligations to practice their disciplinary specialties in hospitals and health organizations that go beyond that required of most other faculty. Academic medicine and dentistry draw from the same organizational structure; faculty and administrative skill set; and issues, challenges, and trends as higher education in general (AAMC, 2008a). These issues include a baby boom bulge of faculty nearing retirement, issues relating to the uncapping of the retirement age, and an influx of younger faculty (male and female) who want improved work–life balance (AAMC, 2008a; Trotman, Haden, & Hendricson, 2007). In these regards, lessons learned from how academic medicine and dentistry address family-friendly policies are applicable to higher education.

The Survey of Deans of Medical and Dental Schools

The deans of the medical and dental schools of the United States and Canada were surveyed as part of a larger longitudinal project (see the Acknowledgments at the end of the chapter). The purpose of the larger study was to examine leadership development among female academics and to evaluate the effectiveness of the Hedwig van Ameringen Executive Leadership in Academic Medicine Program for Women (ELAM), a highly competitive leadership development program for senior female academics in medicine and dentistry in the United States and Canada (ELAM, 2008a; McDade, Richman, Jackson, & Morahan, 2004; Richman, Morahan, Cohen, & McDade, 2001). In 2006, the 206 U.S. and Canadian medical and dental school deans were surveyed regarding work environment, practices used to support leadership development, the existence of family-friendly policies, the impact of ELAM fellows on the school, and the impact of the ELAM program on the ELAM fellows. The responses from the 116 deans, 101 men and 15 women, for a 56% response rate, were representative of the larger population. The methodology for the study is detailed elsewhere (Dannels, McDade, McLaughlin, & Chuang, 2008; Dannels et al., in press).

The Perspectives of Deans

Four themes emerged from our study relating to policies; climate; connections between work climate and policies; and connections among policies, climate, and the increased presence of women.

Family-Friendly Policies

The deans were asked to react to 13 policy categories that are considered family-friendly or gender equitable and to indicate the availability of these policies on their own campus (see Table 7.1). The deans reported a mean number of policies at their schools of 6.11 ($SD = 2.35$). No single policy was universal, and only three were available in more than two-thirds of the schools: paid maternity (91%) and paternity (74%) leaves and benefits for part-time faculty (84%). This upward trend suggests that these benefits may soon become pervasive policies.

In our survey, approximately 45% of medical and dental deans reported five policies at their schools: regular salary equity analysis, optional delayed tenure clock for childbirth or adoption and family needs, nearby childcare, mandated representation of women on search committees, and recruitment of dual-career couples. Fewer than a third of the schools offered tenure for salaried part-time faculty, automatic delayed tenure clock for birth or adoption, incentives to chairs to hire female faculty or to departments for reaching gender goals, automatic delayed tenure clock with special family- needs, or a mandate for at least one female finalist for each search. Barely more than critical mass (i.e., more than 15%) signaled consideration of other family- and women-friendly policies: recruitment of dual-career couples, nearby childcare, automatic delayed tenure clock for childbirth or adoption, and mandated women on search committees. Policies over which deans have

TABLE 7.1

Deans' Perspectives on Existence of Flexibility Policies and Benefits within U.S. and Canadian Medical and Dental Schools

Policy or Benefit	Schools With Policy or Benefit %	Considering %	Do not have %	N/A
Paid maternity leave for faculty	91.2	0.9	6.2	1.8
Benefits for faculty who are salaried part time (e.g. > 0.5 FTE and < 1.0 FTE)	84.1	5.3	9.7	0.9
Paid paternity leave for faculty	74.1	3.6	19.6	2.7
Schoolwide salary equity analysis with report to faculty, annually or biennially	54.5	12.5	26.8	6.3
Optional delayed tenure clock with childbirth/adoption	54.1	12.8	15.6	17.4
Childcare facility at the school or within easy commuting proximity	50.0	17.9	27.7	4.5
Search committees have mandated representation or minimum number of women	40.7	15.0	41.6	2.7
Policies to recruit dual-career couples	40.7	19.5	33.6	6.2

TABLE 7.1 (Continued)

Policy or Benefit	Schools With Policy or Benefit %	Considering %	Do not have %	N/A
Optional delayed tenure clock with special family needs (e.g., care for elderly parents)	43.1	13.8	29.4	13.8
Tenure for faculty who are salaried part time (e.g., > 0.5 FTE and < 1.0 FTE)	30.4	2.7	57.1	9.8
Automatic delayed tenure clock with childbirth/adoption	20.2	16.3	48.1	15.4
Incentives to chairs to hire female faculty	12.6	13.5	69.4	4.5
Incentives to departments for reaching gender work environment goals	8.9	11.6	75.9	3.6
Automatic delayed tenure clock with special family needs (e.g., care for elderly parents)	11.9	13.9	56.4	17.8
Have mandate for at least one female finalist for each search	4.4	11.5	79.6	4.4

N = 116

control—incentives to chairs to hire female faculty or departments for reaching gender work environment goals, and mandates for female finalists in searches—are rare at medical and dental schools. Deans and their institutions seem open to considering new policies, but policy enhancement proceeds slowly.

Work Climate

Because people reach deanships only after many years working their way through faculty and administrative ranks, they have sufficient experience within the academy to compare work climate over time. The deans perceived that the work climate of their schools is better now than 10 years ago. Female deans felt particularly strong about this claim (Likert scale of 1 = strongly disagree to 7 = strongly agree; $M = 5.97$ for all deans, $M = 6.27$ for female deans), which suggests that there has been a noticeable shift in the work climate. Only 6% of the deans disagreed at some level that the work environment had improved, whereas 85% agreed that it had improved. (See Table 7.2.) Although the perceptions of the deans regarding equity may be different from those in the ranks below them, the fact that men and women deans agreed that the climate has improved gives credibility to this claim.

When asked specifically about whether the faculty work environment had improved specifically for women, 91% of the deans agreed that it had improved. Also with moderate agreement (71%), they believed that their own schools have more positive work climates than do other schools (20% neither agreed nor disagreed, and 4% disagreed). Although a substantial number of deans noted that their schools regularly reported (annually or biannually) on the status of women at their institutions, their moderate agreement that the climate at their own schools was more positive for women than at other schools may indicate that they believe that their own school is an anomaly rather than indicating confidence of an environmental shift.

The deans saw areas for improvement. They moderately agreed that gender equity was enforced regarding salary, that there were adequate collegial opportunities for women, and that men and women have equal access to resources. The deans did not feel that men received preferential promotion or had more authority necessary for leadership. In contrast, there was not a consistent agreement regarding statements about women in the workplace, such as on representation of women in senior positions, attitudes toward women, relative attention to men versus women in meetings, and time

TABLE 7.2
Deans Perceptions of the Organizational Climate

Perceived Organizational Climate	Valid Percent*						
	←Strongly Disagree					→Strongly Agree →	
	1	2	3	4	5	6	7
My school has a more positive work environment for faculty now than 10 years ago	0	2.7	3.6	4.5	11.8	38.2	39.1
My school has a more positive work environment for women now than 10 years ago	0	0	1.8	2.7	6.3	45.94	3.2
Compared to other medical schools, our school has a more positive work environment for women	0	0.9	2.8	21.1	14.7	34.9	25.7
My school enforces gender equity with regard to salary	0.9	1.8	3.5	4.4	8	23	58.4
Regular reports (e.g., annual or biannual) on the status of women are important ways to improve the work environment for women	0	1.7	5.2	19.8	16.4	32.8	24.1
My school's environment promotes adequate collegial opportunities for women**	0	0.9	3.4	3.4	19	30.2	43.1
There is equal access for both men and women in lab/research space and resources**	0.9	1.7	10.3	6	9.5	28.4	43.1
Men receive preferential treatment in promotion**	3.4	1.7	5.2	12.1	10.3	24.1	43.1
Men are more likely than women to have the authority that is necessary for a leadership responsibility	0.9	6.2	7.1	10.6	8.8	20.4	46

Women are appropriately represented in senior positions**	16.4	30.2	20.7	2.6	5.2	12.9	12.1
Faculty have a condescending attitude toward women**	8.6	23.3	34.5	11.2	7.8	12.1	2.6
Only time is needed to improve the *institutional work environment* of women, even though nationally over 40% of M.D. graduates are women	7	14	16.7	11.4	15.8	26.3	91.2
Only time is needed for women to move into *leadership positions* within my school, even though nationally over 40% of M.D. graduates are women	8	13.3	16.8	6.2	17.7	24.8	13.3
In meetings, people pay just as much attention when women speak as when men do**	3.4	8.6	10.3	6	8.6	26.7	36.2
Men are more likely than women to receive helpful career advice from colleagues**	3.4	12.9	15.5	20.7	14.7	21.6	11.2

*Responses from 7-point Likert scale where 1 = strongly disagree; 2 = moderately disagree; 3 = slightly disagree; 4 = neither agree nor disagree; 5 = slightly agree; 6 = moderately agree; and 7 = strongly agree

**Item derived from University of Michigan NSF ADVANCE 2005 Survey of the Climate for Women Scientists and Engineers (University of Michigan ADVANCE Program, 2007)

$N = 116$

needed to improve the work climate and move women into senior posts. The variation regarding such statements may have much to do with sensitivity and powers of observation borne from experience that may be gender based.

In summary, the deans, male and female, shared a perspective that faculty work climate has shifted to a positive degree, but there was variability on other issues. The deans perceive the climate to be improving; deans (who are still predominantly male) register that more women are needed in senior posts, that time will help accomplish this, and the climate will then improve to an even greater degree. However, the deans perceive that improvements still are required beyond what the simple passage of time can accomplish. In particular, male deans may still be missing the subtle discrimination that women endure in terms of being noticed and being taken seriously in the work environment.

Connections Between Work Climate and Family-Friendly Policies

The relationship between the work climate and the presence of family-friendly policies is unclear. One would expect that institutions with more family-friendly policies would have a more positive, gender-equitable climate. However, this positive linear relationship is not borne out in the data. When the schools were ranked from low to high by deans' rating of the work climate, unexpected differences arose regarding the prevalence of family-friendly policies. (See Table 7.3.) For example, schools in the upper range of climate perceptions were more likely to have either an automatic or optional delay of tenure clocks for family needs and were more likely to provide paid paternity leave for faculty, but were less likely to provide benefits for part-time faculty. Schools in the upper and lower groups were less likely to provide paid maternity leave and childcare, but more likely to report on salary equity analyses, to have mandated membership of women on search committees and finalists in search pools, and to recruit for dual-career couples than those schools in the middle group. Schools in the lower climate group were less likely to have automatic delayed tenure clock with birth or adoption of children but higher likelihood of optional delay, and they were more likely to provide tenure consideration for part-time faculty. In a number of instances for this sample, the upper and lower climate groups acted more in concert with each other than with the middle group. At least for this sample, there appears to be no relationship between whether a school is perceived by

TABLE 7.3

Schools with Policy or Benefit Considered in Relationship to Standing on Climate Issues

Policy or Benefit	Consideration by Status on Climate by Range of Climate Perceptions (%)		
	Lower n = 19	Middle n = 75	Upper n = 19
Benefits for faculty who are salaried part time (e.g. > 0.5 FTE and < 1.0 FTE)	84.2	85.3	77.8[1]
Paid maternity leave for faculty	84.2	94.7	83.3[1]
Paid paternity leave for faculty	72.2[1]	73.3	77.8[1]
Schoolwide salary equity analysis with report to faculty, annually or biennially	63.2	50.7	64.7[2]
Optional delayed tenure clock with childbirth/adoption	58.8[2]	52.7[1]	52.9[2]
Childcare facility at the school or within easy commuting proximity	44.4[1]	52.0	44.4[1]
Search committees have mandated representation or minimum number of women	47.4	37.3	50.0[1]
Policies to recruit dual-career couples	31.6	44.0	33.6[1]
Optional delayed tenure clock with special family needs (e.g., care for elderly parents)	47.1[2]	37.8[1]	58.8[2]

TABLE 7.3 (Continued)

Consideration by Status on Climate by Range of Climate Perceptions (%)

Policy or Benefit	Lower $n = 19$	Middle $n = 75$	Upper $n = 19$
Tenure for faculty who are salaried part time (e.g., > 0.5 FTE and < 1.0 FTE)	47.4	25.7[1]	33.3[1]
Automatic delayed tenure clock with childbirth/adoption	6.3[3]	22.2[3]	25.0[3]
Incentives to chairs to hire female faculty	11.1[1]	13.5[1]	11.1[1]
Incentives to departments for reaching gender work environment goals	16.7[1]	9.3	11.1[1]
Automatic delayed tenure clock with special family needs (e.g., care for elderly parents)	14.3[4]	8.5[3]	25.0[3]
Have mandate for at least one female finalist for each search	10.5	4.0	11.1[1]

1. 1 missing observation,   2. 2 missing observations,   3. 3 missing observations;   4. 4 missing observations

The groups are formed by dividing the sample by +/− one standard deviation from the mean of the composite score of the environmental climate. Upper and lower = 19 cases each, middle = 75 cases. Seven items in the survey were used from the University of Michigan NSF ADVANCE 2005 Survey of the Climate for Women Scientists and Engineers (University of Michigan ADVANCE Program, 2007). Cronbach alpha = .76.

its dean to have a positive work climate and the specific package of policies and benefits oriented toward family friendliness. Instead, there are a range of policies, and these are idiosyncratically adopted by schools. There is not yet a consensus as to which policies are the most important or necessary, nor any linkage of policies into clusters.

No particular cluster of policies or benefits seems to drive climate improvement, and the sheer accumulation of policies and benefits taken together does not produce a perception of improved climate. Climate and family-friendly policies and benefits are not in sync, which suggests the possibility of an indirect or a mediated relationship. One possibility is that it is not so much the presence of family-friendly policies but more precisely the use of—or the perceived ability to use—these policies without concern for career repercussions that is of importance. The implication for practice may be that merely increasing the number of family-friendly policies may not directly produce the desired improved work climate (Committee on Science, Engineering, & Public Policy, 2007).

The Connection of Policies to Climate and the Presence of Women

The relationship between the existence of family-friendly policies and benefits, work climate, and the presence of increased number of women in faculties is not yet clear. The data show that over the same time span that the number of women on campus has increased, the perceived work environment has also improved. The critical-mass framework offers one interpretation for the work climate and policy advancements. The theory would suggest that the increase of women in faculty and administrative posts within medical and dental schools over past years have driven work climate improvements and the orientation to more family-friendly policies. Perhaps the growing numbers of women faculty (30% in dentistry, 34% in medicine) above the 20% critical-mass level set by Kanter (1977) have been sufficient to drive change. As the numbers of women and younger faculty of both genders in these schools increase, they will have a voice arising from their increasing critical mass. They will expect and call for family-friendly and gender-supportive policies, thus causing more such policies to be put into place, which in turn will make it easier for women to enter and stay in the academy. Conversely, the improved work environment and addition of family-friendly policies may have been responsible for the increase in women in academic medicine and dentistry.

This study does not clearly show whether the increased number of women in leadership positions makes a difference in the advancement of climate and family-friendly policies and benefits. The study found no significant differences between the policies and benefits available at schools led by male versus female deans (or by schools ranked high or low in National Institutes of Health [NIH] funding). The study did not evaluate the gender composition of the administrative hierarchy—only the gender of the dean. The dean alone cannot implement many of the policies and benefits evaluated. We did not probe to connect family-friendly policies to gender composition of schools' senior leadership, to the ability of women to be attracted to or ascend into leadership posts, to acquire the necessary credentials or reputation to ascend into leadership jobs, or for any tipping point at which the lack of family-friendly policies holds back women from ascending in leadership. Not finding or exploring these differences does not mean that they do not exist or do not play a role in the reality and implementation of family-friendly policies and work climate. In summary, a clear relationship has not been shown among work climate, presence of or number of family-friendly policies, and clustering of policies. It is also not yet clear whether the relationship of critical mass of female faculty or senior administrators is direct, mitigated, or irrelevant.

Considerations for Deans

At their heart, family-friendly policies have to do with hiring and retaining faculty and providing a satisfactory work climate that enables faculty to do their best work for the benefit of their school and institution. Such responsibilities sit squarely within the realm of deans (Tucker & Bryan, 1991; Wolverton, Gmelch, Montez, & Nies, 2001). Beyond the data from this study of the perceptions of deans of medical and dental schools, considerations emerge regarding the role of deans, in general, regarding family-friendly policies and their intersection with faculty work climate. The AAMC estimates that "turnover costs [relating to faculty] can exceed $3 million annually at an individual school" (Kirch, 2008). In a competitive faculty environment, any issues are worth consideration and could be considered best practices for deans.

Implement competitive strategies for hiring and retaining faculty. The deans in this study perceived that their own schools had better work climates and family-friendly policies than did competitor schools. Despite conflicting reports connecting family-friendly policies to work climate, deans should be proactive to ensure faculty retention with family-friendly policies because the investment in such policies is likely to be more cost effective than the costs regarding the annual turnover of faculty.

Ensure a positive work climate. A positive work climate is vital if faculty members are to do their best work. The AAMC (2008b) reported that more than 40% of faculty left over a 5-year period; faculty do not wait to see whether climate improves before leaving. If deans perceive any real or imagined relationship of family-friendly policies to climate and faculty retention, they are more likely to advance such policies.

Provide an equitable and fair work environment with congruence between policy and climate. Climate cannot be positive if all employees do not know about, have access to, or feel that they can take advantage of policies that will improve their work lives. Although this study showed that family-friendly policies exist in medical and dental schools, Bunton and Mallon (2007) documented that few faculty use these policies. Deans must not only ensure the existence of such policies but also effect organizational change to remove barriers to their use. Deans can be at the forefront of such changes by mobilizing faculty within their schools who can be change activists. In academic medicine and dentistry, for example, deans could tap alumni of leadership and management programs such as ELAM (2008a) to engage them in devising ways to change internal operations and expectations so as to better align policies and climate.

Collect data regarding the status of faculty. To benchmark and monitor the climate in their schools, deans should collect data about work conditions, implementation of policies, and job satisfaction to understand why faculty start, stay at, or leave jobs. From this study, only 55% of schools conduct an annual or biennial analysis of salary equity, an obvious way to collect data on this aspect of the work climate. Deans can also benchmark faculty employment policies against other organizations in which their faculty could be enticed to work. The usage below 20% for four family-friendly policies and below 30% for another five policies may mean that the schools in this study may not be competitive against other organizations that employ such policies, and this may significantly challenge faculty hiring and retention. Deans can play key roles in establishing the need for evidence, the resources to track data over time, and the use of evidence to support decision making regarding the connection of family-friendly policies and work climate.

Advocate for policies on behalf of faculty and work climate. Deans bear a responsibility to advocate to the larger institution regarding the needs of faculty. Although human resources policies are typically created at the institution level rather than the school level, such policies come into existence because of advocacy—and deans are among the most powerful individuals in a university. Although we found no consistent set of policies adopted across schools, the total number of policies adopted by individual institutions is slowly growing, given that an average of 13.5% of the schools were considering adding at least one new policy. As these schools are embedded in the framework of institutions, the findings in this study mean that there is probably a paucity of such policies across higher education institutions. Banding together, deans across schools can deliver a powerful message to their institutions about the importance of these policies.

Expand the conceptualization of what constitutes family-friendly policies. Leaders should question assumptions and reframe problems (Avolio & Bass, 2002). Deans can play a key role in expanding the concept of what constitutes family-friendly policies and who should use such policies within their schools and institutions. The support of human capital is not just a "woman's thing." Today's family-friendly policies serve both men and women (for example, 74% of the schools in this study offer paid paternity leave) or are gender neutral. As men take on more family and parental care tasks, nearby childcare, delayed tenure clock options for tending to family needs such as elder care, and benefits for salaried part-time faculty will have broader meaning. Benefits for part-time faculty will become more important with the aging of the faculty and the need to retain senior faculty who wish to work part time. As more men of younger generations take on family responsibilities, they will want access to more of these policies that will drive the demand curve for more policies (Lancaster & Stillman, 2003).

Conclusion

Deans play crucial roles in advancing the faculty work environment. This study provides insights from deans of academic medicine and dentistry schools regarding their perceptions of the climate and policies of their schools. In general, they see improvements in the adoption of family-friendly policies and in the work climate in their organizations, although they also report that it will take time for more improvements to solidify. As the policies that schools of medicine and dentistry use are those of the larger institutions in which these schools are embedded, the perceptions of these deans provide instruction for the rest of higher education. Time alone will not be sufficient to make the academic work climate the most positive that it can be. Additional efforts will be needed. Deans can and should play greater roles in ensuring these changes.

Acknowledgments

This research was supported in part by grants from the Robert Wood Johnson Foundation and the Jessie Ball duPont Fund, as well as support from the Mayo Medical School, the University of Michigan Medical School, the Vanderbilt University School of Medicine, and the Wright State University School of Medicine. None of the sponsors had a role in design and conduct of the study; collection, management, analysis, and interpretation of the data; or preparation, review, or approval of the manuscript. We would like to acknowledge Page S. Morahan, Katharine A. Gleason, Victoria C. Odhner, and Rosalyn Richman of the ELAM Program for their contributions to research administration; and several graduate students, Jean McLaughlin, Yu-Chuan Chuang, and Brian Sponsler, at the Center of Educational Leadership and Transformation at The George Washington University, for their assistance in data survey development and data verification.

References

American Council on Education. (2005). *An agenda for excellence: Creating flexibility in tenure-track faculty careers.* Washington, DC: Author.

American Council on Education. (2007). *The American college president: 2007 edition/20th anniversary.* Washington, DC: Author.

American Dental Education Association (ADEA). (2007). Dental students by gender: Trends in dental education (keyword = student by gender). Retrieved June 8, 2008, from http://www.adea.org/

American Dental Education Association (ADEA). (2008). Dental faculty pipeline (gender): Trends in dental education (keyword = faculty by gender). Retrieved June 8, 2008, from http://www.adea.org/

Association of American Medical Colleges (AAMC). (2007a). U.S. medical school faculty, 2007: Table 1: Distribution of U.S. medical school faculty by department. Retrieved June 20, 2008, from http://www.aamc.org/data/facultyroster/usmsf07/07Table1.pdf

Association of American Medical Colleges (AAMC). (2007b). Women in U.S. academic medicine statistics and medical school benchmarking 2006–2007: Table 1: Medical students, selected years, 1965–2007, and Table 3: Distribution of faculty by department, rank, and gender, 2007. Retrieved June 9, 2008, from http://www.aamc.org/members/wim/statistics/stats07/start.htm

Association of American Medical Colleges (AAMC). (2008a). The long-term retention and attrition of U.S. medical school faculty. *Analysis in Brief, 8*(4), 1–2.

Association of American Medical Colleges (AAMC). (2008b). The successful medical school department chair: A guide to good institutional practice. (Including learning modules and suggested readings by topic.) Retrieved June 15, 2008, from http://www.aamc.org/members/msmr/successfulchair/start.htm

Avolio, B. J., & Bass, B. M. (2002). *Developing potential across a full range of leadership.* Mahwah, NJ: Erlbaum.

Broad, M. C. (2005). Filling the gap: Finding and keeping faculty for the university of the future. In R. L. Clark & J. Ma (Eds.), *Recruitment, retention, and retirement in higher education—building and managing the faculty of the future.* Conference Volume: TIAA-CREF Institute Series on Higher Education. Northhampton, MA: Elgar.

Bunton, S. A., & Mallon, W. T. (2007). The continued evolution of faculty appointment and tenure policies at U.S. medical schools. *Academic Medicine, 82*(3), 281–289.

Clark, R. L. (2004, April). *Changing faculty demographics and the need for new policies.* Paper presented at the meeting for the TIAA-CREF Institute Conference, New York, NY.

Committee on Science, Engineering, & Public Policy. (2007). *Beyond bias and barriers: Fulfilling the potential of women in academic science and engineering.* Washington, DC: National Academies Press.

Dannels, S. A., McDade, S. A., McLaughlin, J., & Chuang, Y. (2008, April). *Gender equity, leadership development, and the impact of ELAM: A survey of medical and dental school deans.* Paper presented at the annual meeting of the American Education Research Association, New York, NY.

Dannels, S. A., McLaughlin, J., Gleason, K. A., McDade, S. A., Richman, R., & Morahan, P. S. (in press). Medical school deans' perceptions of organizational climate, advancement of women faculty, and the impact of a leadership program for women. *Academic Medicine.*

Ely, R. (1995). The power in demography: Women's social constructions of gender identity at work. *Academy of Management Journal, 38*(3), 589–634.

Executive Leadership in Academic Medicine (ELAM). (2008a). Web site home page. Retrieved June 8, 2008, from http://www.drexelmed.edu/elam/AboutELAM/home.html

Executive Leadership in Academic Medicine (ELAM). (2008b, February). Women medical, dental and public health deans in the U.S. and Canada to February 2008. Unpublished manuscript, Drexel University, College of Medicine.

Hoffer, T. B., Welch, V., Jr., Webber, K., Williams, K., Lisek, B., Hess, M., et al. (2006). *Doctorate recipients from United States universities: Summary report 2005.* Chicago: National Opinion Research Center. Retrieved June 15, 2008, from http://www.norc.org/nr/rdonlyres/c22a3f40-0ba2-4993-a6d3-5e65939eedc3/0/06srrevised.pdf

Kanter, R. M. (1977). Some effects of proportions on group life: Skewed sex ratios and responses to token women. *American Journal of Sociology, 82*(5), 965–990.

Kirch, D. G. (2008, February). A word from the president: "The state of the faculty." *AAMC Reporter.* Retrieved June 15, 2008, from http://www.aamc.org/newsroom/reporter/feb08/word.htm

Kirch, D. G., Grigsby, R. K., Zolko, W. W., Moskowitz, J., Hefner, D. S., Souba, W. W., et al. (2005). Reinventing the academic health center. *Academic Medicine, 80*(11), 980–989.

Lancaster, L. C., & Stillman, D. (2003). *When generations collide: Who they are. Why they clash. How to solve the generational puzzle at work.* New York: HarperCollins.

McDade, S. A., Richman, R. C., Jackson, G. B., & Morahan, P. S. (2004). Effects of participation in the Executive Leadership in Academic Medicine (ELAM) Program on women faculty's perceived leadership capabilities. *Academic Medicine, 79*(4), 302–309.

National Center for Education Statistics. (2008, March). Digest of education statistics: 2007: Table 239: Full time instructional faculty in degree-granting institutions, by race/ethnicity and residency status, sex, and academic rank: Fall 2003 and fall 2005. Retrieved June 16, 2008, from http://nces.ed.gov/programs/digest/d07/tables/dt07_239.asp?refe rrer=list

Richman, R. C., Morahan, P. S., Cohen, D. W., & McDade, S. M. (2001). Advancing women and closing the leadership gap: The Executive Leadership in Academic Medicine (ELAM) program experience. *Journal of Women's Health and Gender-Based Medicine, 10*(3), 271–277.

Schuster, J. H., & Finkelstein, M. J. (2006). *The American faculty: The restructuring of academic work and careers.* Baltimore: Johns Hopkins University Press.

Trotman, C.-A., Haden, N. K., & Hendricson, W. (2007). Does the dental school work environment promote successful academic careers? *Journal of Dental Education, 71*(6), 713–725.

Tucker, A., & Bryan, R. A. (1991). *The academic dean: Dove, dragon, and diplomat* (2nd ed.) Washington, DC: ACE/Greenwood.

Wolverton, M., & Gmelch, W. (2002). *College deans: Leading from within.* Westport, CT: Oryx Press.

Wolverton, M., Gmelch, W. H., Montez, J., & Nies, C. T. (2001). *The changing nature of the academic deanship.* ASHE-ERIC Higher Education Report No. 28(1). San Francisco: Jossey-Bass.

8

FAMILY-FRIENDLY ACTIVISM

Jeni Hart

Although the creation, implementation, and promotion of the use of family-friendly policies throughout higher education without retribution should simply be the right thing to do, many campuses have not fully embraced these notions. As a result, many campuses continue with the business-as-usual approach and fail to foster a culture where family is a valued aspect of faculty life.

Wolf-Wendel and Ward (2006) explored the nature of family-friendly policies and how they are perceived by faculty in a variety of institution types. They found that across institutional types, there is "a rather tenuous policy environment with regard to work and family" (p. 66). This finding suggests (as do a number of the chapters in this text) that there is still a great deal of work that needs to be done in order to truly call our campuses family friendly. Others (e.g., Coiner, 1998; Drago, 2007; Kolodny, 1998) have identified specific recommendations for creating a work environment that is family friendly, and often the assumption is that it is up to the institutional policy makers to make this happen. To wait on policy makers to "get it" and do the right thing may mean that a family-friendly culture is not likely to emerge any time soon. As a result, some faculty have created grassroots activist networks to put family-friendly issues on the institutional agenda and to ensure that policies and practices are created, implemented, and promoted.

The purpose of this chapter is to share how faculty in two grassroots faculty organizations have pursued a family-friendly agenda that resulted in positive changes on their campuses related to their work. Without the grassroots activism of these feminist faculty, it is unlikely that either campus would have established particular policies and practices. Moreover, the faculty in each organization employed different strategies to advance their family-friendly goals. These two different paths of family-friendly activism can help existing and aspiring activists think of new approaches to push their campuses to become more family friendly. What follows is an explanation of grassroots activism; the background of and context for two grassroots faculty organizations, one at the University of Arizona and the other at the University of Nebraska; descriptions of the family-friendly issues salient for each organization and the strategies used to address their issues on campus; and recommendations for specific strategies that other activists may want to consider as they advance their own family-friendly agendas.

Specifically, activism is considered grassroots when it emerges organically. Rather than engaging in the formal structure of an institution in order to influence decision-making and change efforts, grassroots activism comes from community members who mobilize to address an issue. Although grassroots activism can be an individual activity, this chapter focuses on the grassroots activism of collectives that come together to address feminist issues, including trying to foster a family-friendly climate. There certainly are organizations on many campuses that are interested in family-friendly policies and practices. For example, committees on the status of women are often allies of the family-friendly movement. However, these groups are quite a bit different from the grassroots networks described. Status-of-women committees are generally embedded in the institutional structure and serve at the request of an institutional leader such as the president or provost. As a result of their position within the structure of the institution, the members of the committees are often beholden to the will of the administration (Glazer-Raymo, 1999). Although their efforts may be considered activist, because of the organizations' location within the institutional bureaucracy, they are not grassroots. Grassroots activist organizations may work with the university or college administration; however, their members see themselves as "insiders without." This is to say that they are employed by the institution, but they are working outside the organizational chart to advance issues on their agendas.

Often, as was the case with the women in both organizations described in this chapter, the service in which these grassroots activists engage does not "count" in the same way that serving on a formal university committee, on the faculty senate, or in a professional organization does. Because they are the "insiders *without,*" their activism is not formally rewarded or recognized. However, whether their activism is ever formally rewarded in the promotion, merit, or tenure processes is not the central issue. The issue is that grassroots faculty activists care about their institutions and are working locally to better them. Further, their passion for working on a campus that is family friendly drives them to continue to push forward their agendas to establish policies and practices that promote work–life balance.

Context of the Study

The concepts highlighted in this chapter are primarily drawn from an exploratory qualitative study[1] conducted in 2001. For that research, a comparative case study design was used to intensively investigate two feminist faculty organizations at two large public universities. This analysis allowed me to group together perspectives from interviews, observations, and documents from each organization to shape the themes that guided my research (Patton, 1990). Two feminist faculty organizations served as the foundation of the study: the Association for Women Faculty (AWF) at the University of Arizona (UA) and the Faculty Women's Caucus (FWC) at the University of Nebraska, Lincoln (UNL). First, the background of AWF will be shared, followed by the early history of FWC.

On a sunny afternoon in 1982 in Tucson, Claudia Macintosh called some like-minded colleagues for lunch. Claudia was the director of women's studies at UA, and she felt that it was critical that if the academic program was going to become institutionalized, the campus needed another mechanism to address the status of female faculty. The women's studies program could not serve that role. In addition, although the campus had a commission on the status of women, that group was concerned with issues for faculty, staff, and students, and its purpose was to serve at the will of the board of regents and president. Her colleagues saw the need for a collective of feminist faculty activists, and they came together to form AWF.

The purpose of AWF was to give a voice to faculty women and to provide a mechanism to address issues of gender inequity on campus. Quickly, AWF developed bylaws and an organizational structure. The structure of AWF replicated and complemented the university's administrative structure, with an executive board led by a president, vice president, secretary, and treasurer. Members of AWF extended beyond the board, and each paid nominal membership dues. However, the board, not the broader membership, set the agenda and was the activist arm of the organization. Board members were predominantly tenured faculty, and their participation was publicly acknowledged through newsletters and an organization Web site.

The makeup of the board changed over time. Some members would continue their leadership for three or four years at a time and then pull back from the organization temporarily or permanently. Others would stay involved throughout their faculty careers, but at different levels of effort, sometimes serving on subcommittees, other times opting to run for board positions. The faculty came from disciplines and fields throughout campus. Initially, the members were involved in feminist scholarship and teaching, but throughout the organization's history, fewer members self-identified as feminist, despite their commitment to women's concerns.

The early days of FWC in Nebraska were quite similar to those of AWF. As at UA, one faculty member, Beth Newman, galvanized a small group of faculty women to organize a group that would help female faculty get their voices heard on campus. Over coffee in 1988, Beth and her colleagues formed a feminist grassroots organization that had an independent voice and was not responsible to UNL administration, as the campus commission on the status of women was. However, unlike at UA, FWC did not purposefully differentiate its mission from that of the women's studies program at UNL.

FWC did not have dues or even a formal list of members. Unless a member self-identified as affiliated with FWC, she maintained anonymity. This strategy was particularly important for untenured women who might face backlash from colleagues for being connected to a feminist organization. The lack of structured membership was in stark contrast to AWF. Remaining intentionally unstructured created a distinction from, and competed with, the traditional, professionalized university hierarchy. Although the caucus was unstructured, a core group of individuals consistently participated in FWC over time. The core group was critical in sustaining FWC, but it relied on the additional support of more peripheral members to advance its agenda. The more peripheral members chose to participate based on individual passions for an agenda item, and they saw their commitment as finite (i.e., until the issue was resolved).

Both collectives were predicated on commitment to equity for women. Although many issues were important for both AWF and FWC, such as salary inequities and hostile climate, the need for a campus that was more family friendly always played a prominent role throughout the history of both organizations. In this chapter, I share narratives from two participants, one from each organization, to voice the family-friendly issues that were the most salient at the time of the study and how they engaged in activist strategies to move their family-friendly agendas forward. Specifically, their agendas included creating and implementing tenure clock stoppage and modified duties policies, establishing convenient childcare and sick childcare, creating a university work–life office, increasing healthcare coverage, and enacting partner benefits. In addition, I describe the lessons learned from both of these activist organizations and include a list of potential strategies that other faculty, and even nonfaculty, may want to consider as they pursue their own family-friendly activist agendas.

Activist Strategies and Family-Friendly Issues

The following narratives capture the essence of two different feminist faculty activist organizations. Both groups, AWF at Arizona and FWC at Nebraska, are committed to improving the lives of female faculty on their campuses, and a central part of that commitment is an ongoing focus on family-friendly policies and practices. In fact, members of both organizations credit their activism for policy changes that allow for better work, life, and family balance for faculty. However, each organization approaches how it works toward change differently. Neither model is perfect, but both represent possible ways faculty can engage in activism to advance a family-friendly campus agenda.

AWF

AWF uses professionalized activism as its primary activist strategy (Hart, 2005). Its choice of strategies is guided by the three primary aspects of faculty work—teaching, research, and service—that are integral to who they are as professionals. For example, AWF conducts studies that provide empirical evidence about how many faculty members cancel classes when they have children who are ill and cannot go to daycare in order to impress on administrators the need for accessible sick childcare. It also educates administrators and other faculty about issues, such as faculty challenges in managing the tenure and biological clocks simultaneously, through meetings and seminars. And, much like university service, it establishes committees within its organizational structure (e.g., the Family Care Issues Subcommittee) to make recommendations and, in some cases, draft sample policies. Moreover, the relationships it forges with administrative leaders such as the president, deans, and regents (i.e., prestige networking [Hart, 2008]) is central to accomplishing its goals. AWF sees itself as empowering administrators to make critical policy and procedural decisions because of the trust it has established with institutional decision makers.

Olivia, a former AWF president and activist, explained how important it is to communicate with administrative leaders. She emphasized that not only the fact that AWF communicates with decision makers, but how it communicates helps AWF advance its family-friendly agenda.

> I try very much to speak in a communicative way, to be warm and friendly and enthusiastic in what I am propagating. I've been around a lot of feminist scholars and have seen a lot of hostility among feminist scholars to male colleagues. That is really counterproductive. I have always tried to get along well with my male colleagues, which is surprisingly easy because they have no idea what you are really thinking about them if you are just charming. I think, "Those fools, this is revenge. They don't know what I really think about them." . . . You communicate with them like you can really get along with them, then you can really get along with them. I think my whole fundamental strategy as an activist and as a colleague is that you expect the best out of those that you are dealing with, not the worst. . . . You treat them as [though] if they fundamentally got to know you, they would like you and if you got to know them, you would like them. Often you can get a long way on that; and often, you end up liking them.

Through respectful communication with administrators, AWF has been successful at raising the administrative awareness of family-friendly policies and practices. Moreover, AWF meets before each meeting with the president, provost, or board of regents to carefully plan what will be shared. As part of that choreography, AWF prepares detailed data-driven explanations about the nature of its concerns, and also a draft of a potential response to the concerns. Several of the family-friendly policies AWF has tried to influence are described by Olivia in the following narratives.

Stopping the Tenure Clock at UA

Faculty involved in AWF worked diligently to create and implement a tenure clock stoppage policy. The following story shows that this was not an easy task. Some administrators did not see the necessity of such a policy. However, persistence and education moved the university leadership to adopt a tenure clock stoppage policy. Since the initial policy implementation, the university has expanded the policy to allow faculty to stop their tenure clock once each for two children.

> One of the accomplishments of AWF is the creating of the tenure clock stoppage policy for pregnancy and adoption. One of my favorite stories is that in a presentation by AWF about the efficacy of having parental leave and a way of stopping the tenure clock, a feminist dean said that two rational faculty members should be able to plan [to have] their children over summer break or early in the year. She had her two children that way. They were planned early in the summer and she had all summer to take care of them and in the fall they were ready to go off to daycare. She was also the one to argue that you should only have one child while you are planning for tenure, because that is what rational families do. It was this model of how a rational person would time their childrearing, which would be timing their sexual acts, in order to maximize their time at home. So maybe 48 hours after the final exam. . . . Anyway, it was an interesting view, and one we had to confront and dispel in order to get a policy in place. To do so, we kept making presentations that included a recommended policy to administrators and other faculty, and finally the Faculty Senate voted on the policy.

Modified Duties Policy

Olivia shared another family-friendly success that further exemplifies how AWF uses education to advance its agenda. Olivia was identified as a campus resource for faculty when questions came up about family-friendly issues. Although the AWF board ultimately pushed for the modified duties policy discussed next, the work of the subcommittee was public and recognized by other faculty. This outcome of the AWF's activism is important because it makes family-friendly policies more transparent, which can result in faculty becoming more willing to use them without fear of retribution.

> I knew we were successful when we had our Family Care Issues Subcommittee and we were working on the issue of modified duties, and I was chair of that subcommittee. I had women faculty on campus calling me up who had heard about us and our subcommittee saying, "I'm pregnant and my department head is really unsympathetic. What should I do? Does it

mean I need to take an unpaid leave?" I said, "No, you don't. We are working on a new policy so you can alter your duties for a semester, but there are other policies in place you can use now, like the tenure clock stoppage policy." Faculty on campus really saw the organization as a resource. I was really glad as chair of that subcommittee at the time to help them negotiate with their department heads.

Work–Life Office and Childcare

The University of Arizona has a work–life office as part of the university infrastructure. The office has changed and grown over time, and the work of that office is highlighted in Chapter 3. AWF's activist work played a role in the initial staffing and creation of the office. Specifically, the AWF board continued to provide data to the university president to demonstrate the need for such an office on campus. Raising the administration's conscious-ness about childcare and other family-friendly policies was consistently an item on AWF's agenda each semester when it met with the president and provost, and annually with the board of regents. Olivia shared how a consis-tent message with the university decision makers over time can result in change. She also identified some family-friendly issues that have not resulted in action, but remain on the AWF agenda to remind administrators of the importance of a family-friendly campus.

> AWF is continuing to work on advocating for a childcare center on cam-pus. We were the ones who recommended that the university hire someone to focus solely on family care issues for faculty and staff, and they did. Of course, there is still no childcare on campus, so we have to keep pushing in our meetings with the president and board of regents. Our work has resulted in policy changes like the sick childcare policy. Now, there is a number in human resources that you can call and they will find you low-cost childcare when your children are sick and cannot go to their regular childcare facility. Also, this year we met with the graduate school many times and reinforced our position with the president to recommend that the current graduate student leave policy be changed for graduate students. Right now, if students request a leave for the birth or adoption of a child, they lose all their privileges—no library access, no access to university e-mail, no contact with their advisors. This policy basically prohibits stu-dents from making any progress on their degree while they are on mater-nity leave. The policy also doesn't consider same-sex couples, adoption, or

fathers. I'm not sure we've been able to facilitate a change to the graduate leave policy; but at least we caused pause, if nothing else.

The faculty activists within AWF used both professionalized activism and prestige networking to encourage university administrators to create a tenure clock stoppage policy that could be used twice by faculty, to establish a policy for faculty to modify their academic responsibilities temporarily when a child is born or adopted, to institute a work–family office on campus for the entire community, and to create and maintain cost-effective sick childcare. Of course, these successes did not always come easy. In fact, the sick childcare policy was under attack at one time, and AWF had to again push the administration to consider its value. Further, some family-friendly issues, such as access to convenient childcare and family-friendly policy for graduate students to take academic leave, remained unresolved and still on the agenda at the end of this study. But for the feminist family-friendly activists in AWF, their tenacity, attention to detail and data, and positive, congenial approach with university leaders have resulted in a climate where work–life is a little more balanced than in the past.

FWC

Professionalized activism is one aspect of FWC's overall activist strategy. However, as the narrative from Beth, one of FWC's founders, highlights, professionalized activism and prestige networking is rarely enough to move its agenda forward. Instead, the faculty in FWC are activist professionals. This subtle wordplay foregrounds activism for these faculty. They are still very much professionals, like the members of AWF, and juggle their activism and faculty lives, but their activism drives their identities on and off campus. For example, several of the activists are also involved in the Lincoln community's gay, lesbian, and bisexual (GLB) organization, focusing on family-friendly issues outside the university as well. Their strategies include the teaching, research, service sorts of activities like those of AWF, but their strategies extend beyond that to include leveraging the public. They use the press to publicize their position on the need for insurance coverage for birth control; they personally call members of the state legislature to state FWC's sentiments about partner benefits. Ultimately, as the narrative from FWC declared, any means necessary will be pursued in order to accomplish its activist goals.

Although FWC still meets with campus decision makers on occasion, the group also engages in other strategies that put more pressure on the university administration. Beth explains that meeting with administrators has had little influence on FWC's family-friendly agenda, and as a result, it has sought other ways to advance its goals. In the three vignettes that follow, Beth articulated the variety of techniques that FWC members consider in their work as activists.

> No matter what our strategies are, it is always interesting to see how the administration responds. They treat us like terrorists, basically. And their policy is not to negotiate with terrorists. It is so interesting to see how the administration responds to a different group, like the executive committee, which is largely men, but it includes some women. When they raise an issue, it is always, "Let's sit down," and they work with them. It is an entirely different orientation with the Women's Caucus. If the Women's Caucus brings an issue forward, the last thing they are going to do is listen to you, and the only thing they are going to do is lie to you.

Next, Beth shared a story about how FWC has reinforced its views to the public.

> We've written letters. We write resolutions as well. We wrote a letter once just for fun. In the alumni magazine, they had a woman who was the chair of the alumni association. And the headline on the article was, "Just Call Me Chairman." The whole article was saying how she didn't want to be called *chair*, because a chair is a piece of furniture. Instead, she said she wanted to be called *chairman*. We wrote a letter back as a teachable moment for them to publish, basically saying that in case you haven't noticed, many words in the English language have alternate meanings. Then we concluded with a P.S., saying that we hoped no one moves to table a motion at one of your meetings or someone might get hurt. It was really funny. But it was just to raise consciousness and let people know we are there and watching.

As Beth continued to discuss the strategy of leveraging the public, she described the breadth of tactics FWC will consider in order to advance its family-friendly agenda.

> We don't just talk among ourselves. That is what makes the administration so mad; we talk to the broader community. It is the fact that we know the

editorial board at the Lincoln and Omaha papers. And it is the fact that we know senators. It is the fact that we don't just remain cloistered like a lot of academicians that makes them so mad. And we know what is going on. Therefore, it makes it more difficult for them to lie to us, which they do as a general rule all over the place. Anyway, I think we use every strategy we can think of. We are not always coordinated as well as we should be. We are not always able to push with the right legislative people or the right organizations in town. Part of it is because all of us have full-time lives and full-time professions, but I think we have been able to be effective without just being loud noise. At least that is my summary of the organization. We will use any means necessary, short of doing violence to people, at least physical violence. I'm sure we have been psychologically problematic for some administrators and they see us a big headache. My response to that is, "Just do the right thing." If they did, our activism wouldn't be a problem.

The mechanisms Beth described are central to the FWC strategy of leveraging the public. Initially, FWC often meets resistance from the university administration to its issues and strategies, but leveraging the public has shown to result in both raising the consciousness of the larger university community and family-friendly policy changes. Some of those efforts are described in the next section.

Health Care Coverage and Partner Benefits

As just mentioned, the activism of FWC has resulted in family-friendly policy changes. It has also increased the awareness of the campus and surrounding communities of how much further the university needs to go to be family friendly. Beth shared FWC's work on getting health care coverage for birth control and pushing for partner benefits.

The Faculty Women's Caucus has been a very positive force toward work–family issues. For example, we were instrumental in getting a family leave policy for faculty. More recently, the caucus planned to propose a resolution to the Faculty Senate about contraception benefits, affectionately called the "pill bill." Currently, our health plan will not pay for any sort of contraception, but will pay for other drugs like Viagra. In addition, the GLBT concerns group had brought to the caucus a benefits issue that proposed that tuition remission be afforded to domestic partners, not just husbands, wives, and children, as the new policy is currently understood. They asked us whether it was something the caucus might want to act or speak on. It made sense because both of our issues were about benefits to bring those two things together.

Beth continued:

> Through the years, the caucus has been very vocal about the need for domestic partner benefits. This tuition remission policy is the first step toward getting domestic partner benefits. It is a new benefit, so we are speaking up. Here is an opportunity to change something. We know the legislature and regents don't want to change it because once they change the definition of family in one place, they will be vulnerable to changing it in the whole benefits policies. And they don't want to do that.

As with domestic partner benefits, FWC has met roadblocks in its efforts to increase convenient childcare options on campus. However, FWC has no intention of stopping its activist efforts on either issue. In the next section, Beth described what FWC has done to draw attention to the lack of childcare options on campus.

Childcare

In many respects, the childcare situation at UNL is similar to that at UA. Childcare on both campuses is limited. Although Arizona has made progress on other childcare issues such as providing resources for inexpensive care for children who cannot attend daycare or school because of illness, neither campus has provided much in terms of permanent daycare. Beth outlines the lack of campus childcare and FWC's plan to continue to raise this issue. Although not explicitly stated, FWC will likely address this issue through leveraging the public and other activist professionalized approaches, particularly because of the success those approaches have had in other family-friendly areas.

> We have also tried to make the administration pay attention to childcare issues. We need to have some childcare on campus. What we have is very limited. Basically, to take advantage of what we currently have, you have to plan your pregnancy 3 or 4 years in advance to get on the list. I think there are 20 slots, which is nothing for a campus this size. So we continue to raise this issue and the others I've mentioned, until things change. We now have a leave policy, thanks, in part, to our efforts, and it looks likely that we will get insurance coverage for contraception so we can actually

have financial support in planning our families. But we still have a lot of speaking out ahead of us.

Occasional prestige networking, coupled with leveraging the public, has educated administrators, the campus community, and the city of Lincoln about the family-friendly issues that need to be addressed at UNL. In addition, the activist professionals of FWC have witnessed the creation of a leave policy for childbirth and insurance coverage for birth control. Although it appears that AWF has had more success in the area of family-friendly policies and practices, the campuses are quite different. The strategies used on each campus are influenced by the extent to which the university administration is open to working with faculty activists. Success must be measured differently for each organization, and both AWF and FWC realized family-friendly successes and impediments.

Since the time of the data collection for this chapter, changes in family-friendly policies and practices have emerged. For example, the work–life office at UA has grown and become an institutionalized unit on campus; family-friendly work has a formal home as a result. At UNL, some departments and buildings have established lactation rooms. However, a need remains on both campuses for continuing activism around family-friendly concerns. Both Olivia and Beth reflected on this need in their narratives, and even after the passage of time, many family-friendly initiatives remain unexplored. I hope that AWF and FWC have maintained their tenacity over time and are still pushing, in their own ways, for campuses that are truly family friendly.

Strategies for Family-Friendly Activism

This chapter highlighted two different types of faculty activism and strategies that each type of activist organization primarily used to push forward a family-friendly agenda. These are probably not the only strategies that faculty activists use, but there is much to be learned from the professionalized activists and the activist professionals. The narratives of Olivia and Beth and the experiences of other AWF and FWC activists suggest the following possible methods that others may want to adopt or adapt for their own work.

Consider the relationship you have with those who ultimately make decisions for family-friendly policies and practices. The nature of that relationship can inform the strategies you employ. If decision makers see you as facilitating their work and are open to ongoing discussions, professionalized activist approaches may serve you best. However, if decision makers view you as troublemakers and agitators, you may want to consider an activist professional's approach.

When presenting concerns to administrators about the lack of family-friendly resources on campus, provide potential solutions. For example, compile policies or practices from other peer institutions to share with decision makers, or craft your own policy that best fits the needs of your campus.

Faculty, by nature, are prone to seek out evidence. Use this skill to your advantage. Provide as much data as possible to frame the problem. Data-driven decisions are usually better decisions. Use institutional data, collect new data, and push your institution to collect the necessary data to demonstrate the need for new policies and practices.

If your collective has multiple agendas to consider, subcommittees and task forces of a committed few can provide the groundwork for family-friendly causes; from there, the entire group can then leverage the issue. Activist organizations often have several salient issues that need to be pursued. Having a smaller group of individuals who are most interested in a certain topic come together to frame the problem and possible solutions can be both efficient and effective. Then the larger collective can stand behind the work of the subcommittee as the issue is shared with others through prestige networking and/or leveraging the public.

Sometimes activists run up against roadblocks. Don't give up on what you believe. There are other strategies to consider. Stay on message and continue to educate the campus community, including administrators. Go to the papers. Draft a petition and get signatures. Find allies; for example, local, regional, or national groups may want to take up your cause (FWC has leveraged the National Organization of Women in some of its efforts). Call your legislators or board members.

Know how your university works. Is there a chain of command? Do decisions get made on an ad hoc basis? Are there informal networks that operate and circumvent the formal bureaucracy? Are policies made from the top down or the bottom up? Specifically, is each department responsible for its own family-friendly practices and policies, or are decisions made at the university or college level? Being aware of how family-friendly policies and practices are created and implemented is critical. Knowing whom to involve in your activist network and whether that involvement will be embraced or ignored can help you make the best decisions on what strategies to use.

Use education to your benefit. Activism is often about raising consciousness; to do so, present accurate and complete information about the status of family-friendly initiatives on your campus. Sometimes just educating is enough to help decision makers realize that there is an issue related to family-friendly policies and practices on campus.

Conclusion

AWF and FWC have similar goals in terms of creating campuses where work, life, and family balance is a valued priority. However, each grassroots organization has a different approach to reach its goals. The approaches are shaped, in part, by the relationship each group of activists has with its university administrators. For AWF, having a trusting relationship that included ongoing dialogues with the university president fostered professionalized activism and the use of prestige networking. For FWC, the perceived animosity toward the group made it difficult to rely on professionalized activism and prestige networking. Instead, FWC put pressure on the administration externally. It leveraged the public by using the press to advertise its dissatisfaction with the campus status quo. Agitating the administration was a strategy, in the hopes that administrators would be forced to consider different viewpoints (or more specifically, FWC's agenda). In both cases, successes were realized in terms of their family-friendly objectives. Also in both cases, the activist work was far from over. The fact that activism is still a part of the fabric of the campuses is inspiring. Faculty can be agents of change to create, implement, and promote family-friendly policies and practices. The narratives of the brave activists in this study show at least two of the ways that campuses can become friendlier to families.

Note

1. More complete accounts of this study are detailed in other publications (Hart, 2005; 2007; 2008).

References

Coiner, C. (1998). Silent parenting in the academy. In C. Coiner & D. H. George (Eds.), *The family track: Keeping your faculties while you mentor, nurture, teach, and serve* (pp. 237–249). Urbana: University of Illinois Press.

Drago, R. W. (2007). *Striking a balance: Work, family, life.* Boston: Dollars & Sense.

Glazer-Raymo, J. (1999). *Shattering the myths: Women in academe.* Baltimore: Johns Hopkins University Press.

Hart, J. (2005, Summer). Activism among feminist academics: Professionalized activism and activist professionals. *Advancing Women in Leadership.* Retrieved June 7, 2005, from http://www.advancingwomen.com/awl/social_justice1/Hart.html

Hart, J. (2007). Creating networks as an activist strategy: Differing approaches among academic feminist organizations. *Journal of the Professoriate, 2*(1), 33–52.

Hart, J. (2008). Mobilization among women academics: The interplay between feminism and professionalization. *National Women's Studies Association (NWSA) Journal, 20*(1), 184–208.

Kolodny, A. (1998). Creating the family-friendly campus. In C. Coiner & D. H. George (Eds.), *The family track: Keeping your faculties while you mentor, nurture, teach, and serve* (pp. 284–310). Urbana: University of Illinois Press.

Patton, M. Q. (1990). *Qualitative evaluation and research methods* (2nd ed.) Newbury Park, CA: Sage.

Wolf-Wendel, L., & Ward, K. (2006). Faculty work and family life: Policy perspectives from different institutional types. In S. J. Bracken, J. K. Allen, & D. R. Dean (Eds.), *The balancing act: Gendered perspectives in faculty roles and work lives* (pp. 51–72). Sterling, VA: Stylus.

9

FROM ADVOCACY TO ACTION

Making Graduate School Family Friendly

Margaret Sallee, Mariko Dawson Zare, and Jaime Lester

olleges and universities across the country have implemented an array of policies, programs, and other innovative practices to accommodate the life cycles of faculty and staff. Many campuses proudly advertise the availability of childbirth/adoption leave programs for their employees along with additional incentives for faculty, including the opportunity to stop the tenure clock along with a temporary reduction in teaching duties following the birth or adoption of a child (Hollenshead, Sullivan, Smith, August, & Hamilton, 2005). At elite research universities, these policies are now the norm. Despite their sizable presence on such campuses, graduate students are frequently left out of the quest to create a family-friendly campus. In part, this neglect is due to graduate students' lack of employee status. Federal legislation mandates that despite serving as researchers, instructors, and scholars, graduate students are not employees, rendering them ineligible for family and medical leave and other institutional benefits available to staff. The lack of accommodations is particularly troubling given that without the support of similar policies, many students struggle to progress through their graduate degree program. Given that universities have no legal obligation to accommodate the needs of graduate students, many individuals become agents for change on their own campuses to persuade universities to implement family-friendly policies.

The establishment of family-friendly policies for graduate students is critical to their ability to contribute to and succeed in their academic programs. Graduate students often enroll in master's and doctoral programs during peak childbearing years, are often financially dependent on their graduate student (e.g., research or teaching assistant) positions, and are not eligible for the same accommodations as faculty and staff. Given their lack of financial resources, graduate students are in a particularly vulnerable position. Even institutions that offer a protected leave following the birth or adoption of a child may not be able to accommodate the needs of all parents. For graduate students who serve as their family's source of income, taking an unpaid leave of absence may be a luxury they cannot afford.

In this chapter, we discuss the efforts of one small group of graduate students at the University of Southern California who came together as the Women's Concerns Committee to establish family-friendly policies that are traditionally applied only to faculty and staff. After beginning with a brief review of the unique position of graduate students as simultaneously quasi-employees and students, we describe the types of accommodations available to graduate students on campuses across the country. The bulk of the chapter focuses on the efforts of the committee to introduce a series of initiatives to help graduate students balance their personal and professional responsibilities. We conclude with recommendations for those interested in organizing for similar change.

Graduate Students and Institutional Accommodations

Graduate students occupy a nebulous space on university campuses as a result of the diversity of employment opportunities within the university as well as their student status. Some graduate students earn funding and prepare for academic life by working as either teaching or research assistants. These students are often required to discontinue full-time employment outside the university in exchange for mentorship and paid positions with faculty. Others enroll in professional programs (e.g., law students) and may work outside the university with few or no options for paid positions within the university. Regardless of employment status, all of these graduate students, including those who have paid positions within the university, are only considered students. Their university employment does not grant them status as university employees, which limits access to a range of institutional programs and policies that are available to faculty and staff.

University administrators often point to the history of the faculty–student relationship to explain the privileging of student status over employee. In part, employees owe their access to programs and policies to the lobbying efforts of unions. Although faculty and staff at both public and private institutions across the country have the right to form unions, not all graduate students are afforded such a right. For public institutions, the decision is left to the state. The University of Wisconsin, Madison, became the first institution to allow students to unionize in 1969 (Saltzman, 2000). More recently, University of California teaching assistants earned the right to unionize in 1999, becoming part of the United Auto Workers (Saltzman, 2000). In contrast, all students at private institutions are governed by the National Labor Relations Act (NLRA), which maintains that graduate students are faculty-in-training. Despite engaging in teaching and research, the law maintains that such work is necessary for degree attainment and should not be considered employment (Lafer, 2003; Saltzman, 2006). Although the changing economic landscape in higher education has made graduate students a valuable source of inexpensive labor, the NLRA remains insistent that duties fulfilled by graduate students represent an "educational, not economic, relationship to the university" (Saltzman, 2006, p. 52).

Federal legislation holds that graduate students at private institutions may not unionize. Regardless of one's opinions on the rights of graduate students to unionize, this lack of consistency across campuses leaves graduate students at two serious disadvantages. First, because students are not regarded as employees, institutions are not required to extend the same types of accommodations to graduate students as they do to faculty and staff. Second, without the right to unionize, graduate students at private institutions do not have the political power to organize to advocate for their own needs. Accordingly, policies that affect graduate students' contracts—including those that address major life events—are left to the institution's discretion.

Without these institutionalized accommodations, graduate students become increasingly more reliant on the faculty–student mentoring relationship, which is already fundamental to graduate student success (Baird, 1992; Kurtz-Costes, Hemke, & Ülkü-Steiner, 2006). Socialization into the political culture of academia plays a significant role as a student learns to understand the departmental and university expectations of what it means to be a "good student" (Acker, 2001). Faculty advisors guide students through their research, help them obtain funding, and provide recommendation letters for the job market. Because so much of a student's professional development depends on the support and guidance of the advisor, students can find themselves feeling vulnerable when they need any special accommodations and fearful of jeopardizing their relationship with their mentors. Some students hide their family responsibilities or pregnancies rather than risk the disapproval of their faculty advisors. Because of the amount of time that faculty invest in their students, some professors are hesitant to commit to students they believe may be unable to meet the demands of being a successful graduate student (Acker, 2001). Students who have the added responsibilities of childbearing and childrearing may be perceived as less dedicated to their academic goals. Although the mentoring role certainly benefits the student's professional development, it also maintains the institutional status quo (Margolis & Romero, 2001). Reliance on the faculty–student mentoring relationship means that support for students with families will develop only gradually. Responsibility rests on students' abilities to advocate for themselves without risking the support they need from these mentors for academic advancement.

The State of Graduate Student Family-Friendly Policies

Although classified as students, graduate students often share more in common with faculty than with traditional-age undergraduates. According to the 2004 National Postsecondary Student Aid Study, the average graduate student is 32 years old. In addition, about 25% of all doctoral students and one-third of all master's students have at least one child (National Center for Education Statistics, 2005); that is, at least one in four graduate students has a child in the home. Until recently, institutions provided few resources to graduate students with families. Some institutions provide little more than lists of resources for students, whereas others offer paid maternity leave for new mothers. Even among the 62 institutions that belong to the Association of American Universities, an elite body of research universities in North America, the types of policies available differ wildly. For example, 60 institutions (98%) provide housing lists or services to graduate students with families; 53 (85%) provide lists to help students locate childcare. Although most institutions provide information, fewer provide resources. For example, only 31 (50%) offer housing for students with families. Another 31 institutions offer subsidies to help pay for on-campus childcare. Only 16 (26%) offer any maternity leave or parental leave policy. Of those, only 6 institutions offer paid maternity leave (Mason, Goulden, & Frasch, 2007).

Over the past 5 years, research institutions across the country have implemented a range of initiatives designed to help graduate students achieve a balance between their multiple demands. For example, UC Berkeley offers an extension to time to degree for women giving birth or parents coping with the serious illness of a child. Any parent who applies for such an extension may also receive up to 6 weeks of paid leave from his or her teaching or research responsibilities. However, no income replacement is provided if students do not have a fellowship. Paid maternity leave is available only to students who are employed by the university. Princeton University recently made headlines by introducing a series of family-friendly initiatives for graduate students. The institution provides 12 weeks of paid support for new mothers and a release from teaching and other obligations along with an extension of time to degree. Princeton also provides subsidies up to $5,000 per child to help students pay for childcare. In addition to long-term care, the institution provides a range of low-cost backup childcare options for emergency situations, along with a dependent-care travel fund to allow students to attend academic conferences and pay for care for their children. Some may argue that not all institutions have resources like Princeton to provide such comprehensive assistance to their graduate students. However, as UC Berkeley demonstrates, even state institutions facing serious budget difficulties can still provide assistance to students, if the institutional commitment exists.

Although institutions such as Princeton and UC Berkeley have inserted graduate students into the work–family balance dialogue, not all institutions have followed a similar path. Although the support of administration is critical to institutionalize reforms, change can begin with the action of a small group of concerned individuals. We now discuss how the Women's Concerns Committee acted on a set of issues to ultimately transform the culture of the University of Southern California (USC) campus.

The Women's Concerns Committee: Establishing Support for Graduate Student Parents

The Graduate and Professional Student Senate (GPSS) is the governing body for graduate students at the University of Southern California. Graduate students account for half of the total student enrollment. In 2007–2008,

16,500 graduate students were enrolled at USC. Led by an executive board, GPSS is composed of 73 senators from departments and schools across the campus. All money for programming, education, and advocacy comes from the student programming fee that graduate students pay while attending USC. GPSS has maintained a supportive and productive relationship with the campus administration since its inception. For this reason, GPSS takes an apolitical stance toward "such topics as unionization, taxes on graduate stipends, or any other local, national or international political issue" (USC Graduate and Professional Student Senate, 2005). The apolitical nature of GPSS is particularly important when groups, such as the Women's Concerns Committee, seek to challenge campus policies and raise potentially divisive issues.

Although senate meetings provide a forum for votes on topics, most work takes place in committees, including Academic Affairs, Campus Safety, and Student Programming. The Women's Concerns Committee is one such committee. The committee was created in 2003 by the then–GPSS president; its purpose is to serve as the voice for female graduate students on campus. It was initially formed as a response to a group of female graduate students who were seeking to address issues of safety on campus. The creation and integration of the Women's Concerns Committee served as a bureaucratic mechanism to gain access to GPSS funds and to leverage their administrative network. Therefore, the Women's Concerns Committee focuses primarily on advocacy, whereas other GPSS committees focus on providing programming and social events. Since its inception, the committee has particularly focused on the need for policies to help graduate students who are balancing the competing demands of parenthood and academia. The committee has successfully rallied to implement a pregnancy leave accommodation program, institute lactation rooms, and create a support network for graduate student parents on campus. In each case, our grassroots efforts led to substantial change across the campus.

From Family and Medical Leave to Childbirth and Adoption Accommodation

One of the first major initiatives of the Women's Concerns Committee was to establish a family and medical leave policy for graduate students. During conversations in committee meetings, several group members shared personal or anecdotal information about graduate student colleagues who were experiencing unequal treatment following childbirth as well as medical crises. Students recounted stories of graduate students whose teaching or research assignments were discontinued, leaving the graduate student without employment on returning from childbirth. One student's advisor informed her that if she took leave during the semester to get necessary surgery, she would have no position on returning to campus. Other students shared stories of graduate students getting exceptional accommodations, such as being granted fellowships or guaranteed employment on return from maternity leave. The inequities across campus appeared to depend on individual faculty or departmental administrators' opinions on the appropriateness of graduate students having children. The committee believed that without a campus policy, inequities would continue and certain graduate students would be forced to leave school because of a lack of employment and accommodation before and after childbirth, or worse, students would choose not to have a child to ensure successful completion of their degree.

To establish a family and medical leave policy, the Women's Concern Committee reviewed practices at other universities to understand (1) the pervasiveness of these policies on college campuses, (2) the benefits associated with the policies, and (3) legal concerns that arose because of the implementation of these policies. After acquiring an understanding of national practices, the committee shifted its focus to the institution to understand the degree to which graduate students at USC perceived a need for a family and medical leave policy. In conjunction with GPSS, the committee created a campuswide survey with questions such as "Have you taken a leave of absence due to family or medical reasons?" and "What key concerns did you face upon withdrawing for the leave?" Survey responses provided information on the overall need for the policy as well as the specific needs (e.g., health insurance, campus housing, degree progress) for the committee to consider when drafting the policy. Furthermore, one of the women in the group had access to data on graduate students who used the existing temporary degree progress suspension policy. Although the committee was unable to determine the reasons for suspending degree progress, a safe assumption was that some of the students used the policy for medical reasons pertaining to childbirth or adoption. Gathering this information became essential in conversations with the administration. The committee was prepared to answer questions and was able to document the necessity of the leave policy.

After collecting data via the campuswide survey, the Women's Concerns Committee began to draft the graduate student family and medical leave policy. The committee was primarily concerned with drafting a policy that would reflect the various experiences of graduate students throughout the many academic disciplines within the university. For example, graduate students in the sciences would need accommodations for exposure to laboratories with harsh chemicals; graduate students in English relied heavily on competitive teaching assistant positions for employment. The policy needed to be general enough to account for the differences while also providing an effective baseline of protection for graduate students who experience family or medical needs requiring an absence from graduate school and employment responsibilities. Initial drafts of the policy focused on providing a protected leave for graduate students with either family or medical issues. The policy focused on a range of issues, including stipend replacement, maintenance of health insurance and eligibility for university housing, and special consideration of the needs of international students. After meetings with campus administrators, it became clear that passing such an all-encompassing policy was nearly impossible on a campus that, until recently, provided few accommodations to graduate students. Given that peer institutions across the country had recently introduced pregnancy and childbirth accommodations policies for graduate students, the committee narrowed the policy's scope to focus on these life events.

The resulting policy focused on helping students balance a temporary release from academic responsibilities with the arrival of a new child in the home. Provisions included the ability to postpone course assignments and exams for 6 to 12 weeks in the event of prenatal or postnatal complications; the opportunity to reduce status to part time for a semester; the extension of time to degree and associated academic milestones (e.g., qualifying exam, dissertation defense) by one semester; and the maintenance of health benefits and access to other student services during absence. The policy also provided 6 weeks' worth of stipend replacement to students with existing teaching or research assistantships. For students with prenatal or postnatal complications, the committee recommended providing additional financial support on a sliding scale for up to 6 additional weeks. The policy also included a provision that students were entitled to return to the same or similar position on completion of their leave. In recognition of the difficulties that some students face in asking their advisors for time off for the birth of a child, the committee also recommended that the Graduate Student in Residence, a graduate student appointed to represent his or her peers, serve as a mediator between student and advisor.

The committee's policy traveled through different campus committees and underwent several modifications before appearing in its final form as the Childbirth and Adoption Accommodation Program. Not all of the committee's original provisions appeared in the final policy. In addition to earlier concessions with respect to providing medical leave to graduate students, the new program is limited to Ph.D. students only. The policy went from one that provided accommodations for family and medical leave concerns to one that accommodates only graduate students in Ph.D. programs who adopt or bear children while in school. Although not all graduate students can access the new program, it stands as the first time that any accommodation has been systematically offered to graduate students at USC. The program provides academic accommodations, including an extension of the degree clock, maintenance of full-time student status, and for some, stipend replacement. Unlike the committee's final policy, the program provides a stipend replacement for one semester, which allows graduate students to take one full semester off and still receive pay. The graduate school has created a small fund to use to pay a student's stipend or to provide funds to the department to hire a temporary replacement. In this sense, the policy is far more generous that the committee had hoped it could be.

However, the policy has several crucial limitations. First, the pregnancy policy does not accommodate all graduate students. Students who are in master's degree programs or professional doctorates are excluded. Thus, only a fraction of the graduate students at USC are eligible for the accommodations. Although 16,000 degree-seeking graduate students attend USC, only 4,241 (26%) of those are Ph.D. students. Of the remaining students, 57% are enrolled in master's programs; 17% are pursuing a professional doctorate, such as law or medicine (University of Southern California, 2007). Certainly some students enrolled in other types of graduate programs also have children. Yet the policy provides no assistance to these students. Second, although all Ph.D. students are eligible to have their degree progress suspended during their absence from campus, students who do not have a guaranteed funding contract at the time of the birth or adoption of the child may not be eligible for stipend replacement. Many students have only semester-long or yearlong contracts and find it difficult to secure a teaching position in advance of a delivery or adoption date. Third, medical leave was removed from the policy. Although it is important to protect graduate students who bear children or adopt, many other students become ill or need to care for family members who are ill or aging. Without protection, those students have to temporarily discontinue their studies in order to care for themselves or family members with medical difficulties.

Another difficulty arises from naming this provision a "program" rather than a "policy" and the intention to provide the flexibility to accommodate students from a wide range of research and teaching responsibilities. The result is that the program lacks specific details about some of the procedures, often relying on the degree to which students feel comfortable approaching first, the graduate school, and second, their advisor or department, about their need for leave and stipend coverage. This has led to a certain degree of confusion about what students can expect in the way of specific benefits, because each case is uniquely determined. Nonetheless, some students have benefited from this program. The graduate school advises students about how to approach faculty and advisors. Women have been able to maintain their stipends during their childcare leave and have found their funded positions available on their return.

Lactation Rooms

Although the Childbirth and Adoption Accommodation Program provides assistance to new mothers, the need for assistance does not end once a new parent returns to campus. Although the program provides time off to new mothers, many women return to campus while they are still breastfeeding their children. Until recently, the USC campus provided no designated space for women to pump breast milk and willingly paid an annual $500 fine to the State of California for not doing so. For most faculty and staff, this lack of space does not pose a problem because most can use their own offices or a private conference room. However, not all graduate students have dedicated office space. Some students work in labs with other students and staff; other students share office space with several peers. Through our outreach across campus, we heard from women who used a variety of strategies to locate space to pump breast milk. Some negotiated with their department for the use of an empty office, but others found themselves faced with options that were less than sanitary, private, or safe—pumping in bathrooms, the women's locker room of the student gym, or even in their cars. The lack of dedicated space left students with few secure options.

In 2005, the Women's Concerns Committee first started to address the need for lactation rooms on campus. We met with staff in various campus offices to discuss our concern over the lack of space. We were assured that a lactation room was being included in plans for a new campus center, set to open in 2010; however, one lactation room promised for 5 years in the future for a campus of 30,000 students was severely inadequate. As a frame of reference, UC Davis, a campus with 26,000 students, has a breast-feeding support program that operates 33 lactation rooms across its two campuses. Even the provision of one room in the campus center proves helpful only insofar as students can travel to and from the lactation room quickly enough without interrupting their obligations to teaching, research, or coursework schedules. This room would also provide no relief for students spending most of their day at USC's Health Sciences Campuses. Thus, more work was needed to continue to locate viable lactation room spaces.

To address the needs of breastfeeding mothers on campus, we focused on both short-term and long-term goals. Although our ultimate priority was to secure dedicated space, such a process can often be complicated, especially on campuses where space is at premium. We knew of women who needed space to pump immediately and could not wait for a few months, let alone a year, for administrators to open a lactation room. The committee first served as an informal referral service. We posted flyers and sent messages to campus e-mail discussion groups, offering to help women find temporary spaces to lactate. Although we were contacted by several women, all were disheartened to learn of the lack of dedicated space on campus. Having to negotiate with campus staff for a private room in which to pump proved to be too much for many of the women, and all sought other accommodations.

Despite our efforts through meetings with campus administrators to discuss the possibility of finding a dedicated space, no action was taken. Accordingly, we used the graduate student senators to help us find an interim solution. We contacted senators in departments across campus to ask for their help in identifying unused closets or rooms in their departments that might be converted into lactation rooms. Although we received some positive responses from departments, most were only willing to provide temporary accommodation to their own students, rather than permanently convert the space and open it to all in the campus community. Serving as an intermediary for lactating women was never a viable long-term solution. However, our efforts to publicize the need for lactation rooms led the institution to push more actively to create dedicated space on campus. In the 2006–2007 academic year, the vice president of student affairs convened an informal workgroup to identify potential rooms that might be converted to lactation rooms. By the end of the year, two private bathrooms in buildings across the campus were slated to be converted to lactation rooms. The first room opened in the fall of 2007 in the women's locker room of the university gym and includes a door with a lock, a chair, an electrical outlet for the pump, shelving, and hooks for clothing. The dedication of such space is a significant improvement over the committee's efforts to help women on an as-needed basis. All breastfeeding mothers can use the room when necessary as they return to campus while still balancing the demands of having an infant in the home.

Although the campus now has lactation rooms, few women know of their existence. The administration of the lactation rooms is formalized by the oversight of the Center for Work and Family Life. However, the center's Web page contains no information about the rooms. The Women's Concerns Committee has put the information on its Web page and has asked other offices, including the Center for Women and Men and the student health center, to do the same. Without more direct publicity efforts organized by the campus community, support for the lactation rooms seems marginalized to specific student services.

Graduate Student Parent Network

The committee's advocacy led to institutional efforts to provide assistance to new mothers, through both the Childbirth and Adoption Accommodation Program and the dedication of lactation rooms. Despite this assistance, graduate student parents continue to be both an invisible and isolated segment of the campus population. To help foster a sense of support among graduate student parents, the committee started the USC Graduate Student Parent Network (GSPN) in the fall of 2006. Modeled after the Berkeley Parents Network (see the resources in the appendix for more information), GPSN is primarily an online forum that allows all graduate students to have frank conversations with one another about the challenges of being a parent and student. In addition, the online forum allows committee members to distribute information about policies and initiatives that affect graduate student parents. For example, not all graduate students received information about the implementation of the Childbirth and Adoption Accommodation Program or the opening of the lactation room. GSPN provides another avenue to transmit information to students. GSPN maintains an archive of information on these existing services, programs, and facilities, making it easier to continually communicate to the incoming GSPN membership, who may have not been present during the initial publicity.

In addition to serving as an information network, GSPN also functions as a support network. Once a semester, the group hosts a social function for graduate students and their children. Although GSPN began with a small group, membership is steadily growing. Events have been attended by students who are currently parents as well as those who may be expecting babies or contemplating having children while in graduate school. In an effort to provide a space for students to freely discuss their concerns, the GSPN online forum and social events have been useful in providing a peer network that can be supportive and provide mentorship.

Recommendations for Practice

Since its inception, the Women's Concerns Committee has advocated for the needs of mothers on campus. Because of our efforts, the campus now provides assistance to new mothers along with other support to graduate student parents. In this section, we offer recommendations for different populations on campus: for graduate students interested in organizing for change and for administrators who work with graduate students.

For Graduate Students

Organize with a committed core. The Women's Concerns Committee has never been a large committee. Typically, the group has consisted of six to seven committed members with others who show support throughout the year. Despite our small size, we accomplished a great deal by creating a trusting and supportive environment, establishing a leader to set agendas and push forward initiatives, and working with graduate students across the campus. The small group of women met monthly to discuss graduate school, to share personal experiences, and to seek advice on a myriad of topics. These conversations helped to establish trust within the group and build commitment among the team. Furthermore, these conversations led to several of the initiatives as a form of consciousness raising that showed that "the personal is political." For example, the lactation room initiative was started after one of the members described her struggle with finding an appropriate space to pump breast milk. Another important aspect of the committed core was the establishment of a leader. Although this group functioned by consensus, having a defined leader helped keep the group on track by delegating responsibilities and maintaining an agenda. Finally, the group consisted of graduate students from across the campus. The diversity of the group led to the development of creative strategies, extended the network of allies, and helped frame the local experiences of each graduate student.

Get issues on the radar of administrators and graduate student body. One of the major reasons that the Women's Concerns Committee was successful was timing and strategic leveraging of networks. Right before the committee was ready to present the graduate student leave policy to the campus administration, the campus appointed a new vice provost for graduate programs. A woman with a history of advocating for the inclusion of women in science, the vice provost proved to be a strong advocate and lobbied for the passage of the pregnancy policy. Therefore, other groups who are trying to create change need to scan the environment and strategize on changes in the administration, events that bring issues to the fore, or other changes that create the right time to push initiatives forward. Second, the committee has an established informal and formal relationship with GPSS, which had a graduate student representative on the provost's Graduate Student Advisory Committee. By establishing the Women's Concerns Committee as a part of GPSS, the group was able to leverage its status within GPSS to gain support and to find a forum to discuss the policy. Thus, groups need to establish networks with, or become part of, advocacy bodies that have opportunities to present issues to administrators in power. Moving at the right time and with the right actors may lead to success or failure.

Be willing to compromise. Particularly with the pregnancy leave policy, the Women's Concerns Committee had to learn to compromise on its position. As stated earlier, the original intent of the committee was to create a family and medical leave policy that included men and women who were seeking leave for pregnancy, adoption, or illness. When the policy was presented to the provost's committee, it was seen as too encompassing and aggressive. Subsequently, the committee had to make substantial revisions and compromise on the beneficiaries of the policy. Although this was a difficult decision involving many weeks of debate, the committee agreed to the revisions in order to establish an initial policy that could be modified in the future. Graduate student groups and change agents need to consider a compromise in order to establish new policies, particularly around issues that require administrative approval and additional funds.

Consider the campus culture. Every campus has a history and a culture that will impact the success of change agents. The Women's Concerns Committee was working toward change on a campus that has a conservative history and campus climate. Groups seeking change around family-friendly policies need to consider strategies that fit the campus culture. For example, the Women's Concerns Committee leveraged the university's desire to compete with similar institutions as justification for the establishment of the pregnancy policy. Group members examined the practices of other research universities to determine which campuses offer leave policies for graduate students. The committee also conducted a campuswide survey of all graduate students to illustrate the pervasive need for a pregnancy policy and lactation rooms on campus. Having data was important for a campus that relied on data-driven decision making and respected those who developed informed policies. In addition, the committee used strategies that worked within the institutional policies versus direct activism. Rather than protesting the need for pregnancy policies or lactation rooms, the committee worked with GPSS and had conversations with the administration to bring about change.

For Administrators

The recommendations just outlined are important for groups of students who are seeking to establish or extend family-friendly policies and practices for graduate student populations. Inherent in the work toward the establishment of family-friendly policies is a need to work with the campus administration. Therefore, we outline some suggestions for campus administrators to assist in successfully implementing and promoting family-friendly policies.

Fit graduate students into existing resources. Graduate students occupy a unique position on campuses. With different responsibilities from undergraduates yet a lack of legal recognition as employees, graduate students occupy a middle ground between student and staff and are often neglected by campus policies. Although certainly graduate students can benefit from policies designed with their needs in mind, administrators may remember to extend existing campus resources to these students. For example, if lactation rooms are available for all in the campus community to use, extending the right for graduate students to use them costs the campus little.

Disseminate information. Even the best practices will be ineffective if few know of their existence. We are still surprised by the number of students who tell us they do not know about the Childbirth and Adoption Accommodation Program. Relevant programs and policies should be advertised on multiple Web sites, including the graduate school and the institution's work–life balance office, if one exists. We would also suggest establishing links to this information from any gender-based offices on campus, such as women's centers. Further, policies and programs should be regularly publicized via e-mail each year.

Remember the unique needs of different student populations. Graduate students are a diverse student body. Some are on campus for 2 years, seeking a master's degree; others are enrolled in lengthy Ph.D. programs. Still others are earning professional degrees, such as an M.D. or J.D. The Childbirth and Adoption Accommodation Program at USC is designed only to provide income replacement for students enrolled in doctoral programs. One wonders why women who are pursuing a law degree or enrolled in a master's program are less eligible for the same types of assistance. In addition, many research institutions count a large number of international students as part of their graduate student body. Because of restrictions associated with student visas, most international students are unable to take an official leave of absence without leaving the country. In formulating the Childbirth and Adoption Accommodation Program, USC included provisions to allow international students to maintain their visa status and access the program. Similar attention should be given to other vulnerable student populations on various campuses.

Conclusion

The work of the Women's Concerns Committee was instrumental in fostering a campus culture that opened the way for the development of a vibrant and productive discourse on family-friendly practices for an underserved graduate student population at USC. Although the process required patience and perseverance, tangible results can be achieved through dialogue between the graduate student community and the university administration. The small group of dedicated students who formed the committee served as a voice that spoke to the university administration on behalf of graduate students. As a result of their role in the establishment of family-friendly programs for graduate students, the Women's Concerns Committee has become more visible, enabling them to further facilitate the communication of information on existing resources to graduate students with families, as well as the expression of the need for the implementation of other forms of support in the future. Opening these topics for discussion has enabled the implementation of specific programs to serve students, and a discourse has been established that can be built on as the committee continues to serve this population.

References

Acker, S. (2001). The hidden curriculum of dissertation advising. In E. Margolis (Ed.), *The hidden curriculum in higher education* (pp. 61–78). New York: Routledge.

Baird, L. L. (1992). *The stages of the doctoral career: Socialization and its consequences.* Paper presented at the annual meeting of the American Educational Research Association, San Francisco, CA.

Hollenshead, C. S., Sullivan, B., Smith, G. C., August, L., & Hamilton, S. (2005). Work/family policies in higher education: Survey data and case studies of policy implementation. In J. W. Curtis (Ed.), *The challenge of balancing faculty careers and family work: New directions for higher education, no. 130* (pp. 41–65). San Francisco: Jossey-Bass.

Kurtz-Costes, B., Hemke, L. A., & Ülkü-Steiner, B. (2006). Gender and doctoral studies: The perceptions of Ph.D. students in an American university. *Gender & Education, 18*(2), 137–155.

Lafer, G. (2003). Graduate student unions: Organizing in a changed academic economy. *Labor Studies Journal, 28*(2), 25–43.

Margolis, E., & Romero, M. (2001). In the image and likeness . . . : How mentoring functions in the hidden curriculum. In E. Margolis (Ed.), *The hidden curriculum in higher education* (pp. 79–96). New York: Routledge.

Mason, M. A., Goulden, M., & Frasch, K. (2007, May). Graduate student parents: The underserved minority. *Communicator: Council of Graduate Schools, 40*(4), 1, 2, 5.

National Center for Education Statistics. (2005). National Postsecondary Student Aid Study (NPSAS:04). Washington, DC: U.S. Department of Education, Institute of Educational Sciences.

Saltzman, G. M. (2000). Union organizing and the law: Part-time faculty and graduate teaching assistants. *The NEA 2000 Almanac of Higher Education, 43–55.*

Saltzman, G. M. (2006). Rights revoked: Attacks on the right to organize and bargain. *The NEA 2006 Almanac of Higher Education, 49–63.*

University of Southern California. (2007). *At a glance—USC student characteristics.* Retrieved April 14, 2008, from http://www.usc.edu/private/factbook/2008/all_byclass_08.pdf

USC Graduate and Professional Student Senate. (2005). *Statement on the apolitical stance of GPSS.* Retrieved April 14, 2008, from http://www.usc.edu/org/gpss/about_gpss.html

THE FAMILY-FRIENDLY CAMPUS IN THE 21ST CENTURY

Margaret Sallee and Jaime Lester

What began as a small movement several decades ago, isolated to a few institutions, has blossomed into a necessary provision that many colleges and universities are compelled to provide in order to attract faculty and staff in a competitive marketplace. The types of policies available to faculty and staff range dramatically from campus to campus. Some provide little more than unpaid leave following the birth of a child; others offer a whole recipe of policies, including paid leave, a reduction in teaching duties, and subsidized childcare. Although we certainly argue that faculty and staff are better served when they have more policies available to use, such policies may be of little use when there is little institutional support for work–family balance. Rather, as many of the chapters suggest, a successful campus changes its institutional culture to one that values the employee's life demands, both on and off campus. Here, we briefly summarize the changes in the ways in which institutions have thought about work–family balance over the past 50 years along with areas that will receive increasing attention in the decades to come.

Changing Definitions of the Family-Friendly Campus

Although campuses are increasingly expected to be family friendly, such an expectation is relatively recent. As Rosalind Barnett (1999) argues, organizations have moved through three distinct phases of work–family balance.

Although earlier models saw work–family balance as a women's issue, today's models recognize the importance for parents of both genders to achieve a balance between work and family. Barnett characterizes organizations in the 1950s through the early 1970s as adopting a *separate spheres model,* in which women were intended to keep their family responsibilities separate from their professional responsibilities. Women who worked outside the home were expected to leave their family problems outside work and conform to the male norms of the workplace. Some organizations helped women balance their competing demands, but solely in order to increase workplace productivity.

Over the past several decades, there has been increasing recognition that work and family do not reside in separate spheres, leading organizations to adopt what Barnett (1999) labels the *overlapping spheres model.* This model characterizes achieving a work–family balance as an issue for both mothers and fathers. This model posits an interdependence of work and life and does not highlight any conflict between the two realms, in marked contrast to the separate spheres model. Despite the rhetoric, organizations have not responded with policies to help employees balance the separate spheres.

Some institutions have adopted a *work–life integration model,* which operates on the assumption that both male and female employees perform their best when they are involved in multiple spheres. Unlike the separate spheres model, which assumed that women's roles as mothers necessarily conflicted with their roles as employees, the work–life integration model recognizes the interdependence of employees' multiple spheres. An individual's experiences in the home will necessarily impact his or her performance in the office, and vice versa.

A decade ago, Barnett (1999) suggested that institutions should abandon these models in favor of a *work–life systems framework.* In this model, the entire work–life system, not the individual worker, is the unit of analysis. Consequently, organizations are not just concerned with what happens to their employees while at work, but also with their functioning in all aspects of their lives. "Decisions are no longer seen as pitting one person's needs against another's; rather, decisions are made to optimize the well-being of the system" (Barnett, 1999, p. 153). According to this model, workers now become central to the operation of the system. Rather than expecting employees to conform to predefined norms, the organization is expected to work with employees to create mutually beneficial practices. The University of Arizona's Life & Work Connections operates under an integrated, hybrid model that provides assistance to staff throughout the life cycle. The office staff provides a range of services to all in the campus community, regularly collaborating across programs to make sure that the needs of the individual are met.

Like the University of Arizona as described by Jung and colleagues (Chapter 3) and the Johns Hopkins University as outlined by Beauchesne (Chapter 5), other campuses that operate from a systems framework pay attention to the needs of faculty and staff throughout employment. In an ideal world, the campuses would adopt the following practices. To level the playing field, faculty members who have children would be granted some type of assistance to make tenure outcomes more equitable. Such policies would be expanded to address the needs of all faculty on campus. Although achieving tenure removes a significant source of stress for many faculty members, work–life conflicts do not stop at the associate professor level. Many faculty in these positions continue to struggle to balance the demands of work and family. Under the systems model, having and raising a child is not a concern just for the individual faculty member. Instead, it becomes the institution's responsibility to help faculty negotiate the demands of parenthood. Rather than just providing policies that place the onus on faculty, universities can provide resources—such as childcare for young kids or programs for kids of all ages over breaks from school—to allow faculty to integrate their work and family lives. It is our hope that the systems framework becomes the norm across campuses. We now turn from a discussion of past work–family efforts to changes we see on the horizon.

Broadening the Focus of Work–Family Balance

The chapters in this volume highlighted the ways in which colleges and universities have changed their organizational culture to help employees achieve a balance between their personal and professional responsibilities. Certainly some institutions—such as the University of California (Chapter 6) and the University of Washington (Chapter 2)—have a longer history with work–family balance programs that cater to faculty, staff, and students. Other institutions are only beginning to develop programs for faculty; still others are expanding existing policies to incorporate staff and students. The work–family balance movement is gaining increasing acceptance in academe. Many top-tier research institutions offer an array of policies to help recruit and retain faculty. Smaller and less elite institutions are also beginning to offer policies to their own faculty. Over the next several decades, we suggest that the work–family balance movement will continue to change to incorporate new populations, new institutional types, and new policies.

Incorporating New Populations

Typically, tenure-track faculty have been the primary beneficiaries of institutional policies. Programs such as the opportunity to stop the tenure clock and the reduction of teaching duties following the birth or adoption of a child clearly were designed with faculty in mind. However, many institutions offer policies that can be used by all in the campus community. Here we consider how staff, students, and clinical faculty may be incorporated into work–family balance policies.

As many of the chapters highlighted, staff are eligible for a wide range of programs and policies. For example, the University of Washington offers on-campus childcare slots to both faculty and staff. The University of Arizona provides an array of services, including lactation support to all new parents. Many institutions are also experimenting with flexible work arrangements, allowing staff to configure their work schedules to meet the needs of their office as well as their personal needs at home.

Students have only recently been incorporated into the work–family dialogue. In part, this exclusion was based on the assumption that students had no families or personal responsibilities of their own and were not in need of assistance. As the chapter on graduate students highlighted (Chapter 9), institutions have recently started to provide accommodations for graduate student parents, including leave following the birth or adoption of a child and assistance with childcare. However, such assistance varies wildly by institution. Princeton provides a guaranteed semester of paid leave to birth mothers; Stanford provides 6 weeks of paid leave. Other institutions provide no assistance.

Although graduate students certainly can benefit from more institutional assistance, undergraduate students are neglected. In part, these differences stem from employment status. Graduate students are quasi-employees and therefore receive some institutional aid. Undergraduate students are simply students. Although undergraduates are eligible to use campuswide programs (such as lactation rooms and childcare), they are simply incorporated into existing programs, rather than having programs designed specifically for them. As the demographics of the undergraduate population continue to shift from those fresh out of high school to returning adults, we suspect that students will begin to demand more assistance in the work–family arena.

While the undergraduate student population is changing, so is the faculty population. According to the 2004 National Study of Postsecondary

Faculty, 34% of all faculty are employed part time, and 28% of full-time faculty are not on the tenure track. Institutions are increasingly turning to clinical faculty as a cost-saving measure. Clinical and adjunct faculty receive less pay than their tenure-line (tenure-track and tenured) counterparts. More important, because they are not tenured, their positions may be terminated should the department or institution's needs change. Increasingly, clinical faculty are simply viewed as human capital. They are not eligible for the same types of aid as their tenure-line counterparts, including family-friendly benefits. As institutions continue to increase their reliance on non-tenure-track faculty, they will need to find ways to incorporate all faculty—both tenure and non-tenure-line—into the work–family dialogue. Institutions may consider providing a release from teaching duties following the birth or adoption of a child to clinical faculty who have completed a certain number of years of service. The approach will differ by institution. However, campuses must make some effort to assist clinical faculty with achieving a balance between their competing demands, or risk widening the gap between the two types of faculty. For information on how faculty can help to advocate for new policies, see Chapter 8.

Expanding to New Institutional Types

As many of the chapters pointed out, work–family balance policies have become synonymous with research institutions. All of the winners of the 2006 Sloan Awards for career flexibility were research universities (Chapter 1). Only recently has the foundation expanded its awards to recognize and promote family-friendly policies at master's-granting institutions. (Sloan Awards are in their third round directed to liberal arts colleges—first focused on research universities, second on masters, and third on liberal arts). The work of a professor at a liberal arts college differs from that at a research university—liberal faculty focus almost exclusively on teaching and service—which creates different concerns regarding career flexibility (Chapter 4). For example, faculty at liberal arts colleges teach more courses (more than four courses a semester), sit on more service committees, and have a greater time commitment to student populations. In the case of illness or the birth or adoption of a child, departments need to find additional adjunct or teaching substitutes, new ways to staff committees, and other faculty to assist with student needs. These requirements create additional burdens on department chairs and other faculty. Moreover, institutions that already rely on many part-time faculty (e.g., community colleges) who are excluded from governance and other service activities create a heavier burden for those few full-time faculty. When a full-time faculty member needs additional accommodations, there are fewer human resources to fill those gaps in teaching and service. Therefore, institutional accommodations need to be designed with these responsibilities in mind.

Developing New Policies

Most institutional policies are designed to help new parents welcome a child into the home. Parental leave, a reduction in teaching duties, and the opportunity to stop the tenure clock are the standard trio of policies provided for faculty at most research institutions. Although certainly new parents—particularly those who have not yet earned tenure—face multiple demands on their time, faculty in all stages of life can benefit from work–family balance policies. Increasingly, institutions are turning their attention across the life cycle to help faculty who are not just caring for new children, but those caring for aging parents. Many institutions, like the University of Arizona and the Johns Hopkins University, offer elder care programs that help employees develop strategies and identify resources to care for aging parents and other relatives. Institutions may consider introducing policies that provide subsidized short-term and long-term leave for faculty for a variety of life issues, including childbirth, illness, or caring for ill relatives.

In addition to expanding the availability of policies, institutions may also continue to investigate ways to promote flexibility in the workplace. Although faculty members have a great deal of flexibility as to when and where they perform their work, staff members are typically bound by the strictures of the 9-to-5 workweek. Institutions across the country have experimented with flexible work arrangements, including flexibility in the schedule of hours worked, flexibility in the amount of hours worked, and flexibility in the place of work (Workplace Flexibility 2010, n.d.). For example, some institutions allow employees to work a compressed workweek such as completing four 10-hour days, instead of the traditional five 8-hour days. Other employees have more latitude to arrange their schedule around times mutually agreeable between supervisor and employee. For example, some employees may come in before 8 a.m. and leave before 5 p.m. Still others may take a long break in the middle of the day and work later in the evening. Such arrangements allow employees to attend to their personal needs while simultaneously fulfilling professional responsibilities.

In addition to variability in setting hours, some employees may also choose to reduce the number of hours they work, either by working temporarily part time or by engaging in job sharing. Such options are particularly attractive for those who wish to spend more time with a young child or an ill family member. Finally, particularly during an economic downturn, some institutions permit and even encourage employees to work from home. Such an arrangement not only saves the time and money that arises from commuting, but may also allow employees the flexibility to balance their needs. Regardless of the type, policies that encourage workplace flexibility may ultimately lead to more satisfied employees who can participate in both the domestic and academic spheres.

The Family-Friendly Campus in the 21st Century

What began as a recruiting tool for faculty has become standard policy at many research institutions. As the authors in this book have suggested, family-friendly policies are becoming incorporated into the fabric of institutional culture. Such policies are necessary not only for retaining the best talent, but simply as a matter of necessity. Productive employees can devote time both to their personal and professional obligations.

The chapters in this volume have profiled the best practices in family-friendly campuses across the United States. Chapters have considered practices at a variety of institutions and policies that target faculty, staff, and students. We hope that these practices offer administrators, faculty, and other interested parties a blueprint to begin to work for similar changes on their own campuses.

References

Barnett, R. C. (1999). A new work-life model for the twenty-first century. *Annals of the American Academy of Political and Social Science, 562,* 143–158.

Workplace Flexibility 2010. (n.d.). *Flexible work arrangements: The fact sheet.* Retrieved June 1, 2008, from http://www.law.georgetown.edu/workplace flexibility2010/definition/general/FWA . . . FactSheet.pdf

RESOURCES

The following pages contain examples of family-friendly policies from institutions around the United States, organizations that focus on work–life issues, and recent publications and Web sites of interest. By no means is this list exhaustive; it simply provides a starting point for those interested in learning more about the issues discussed in this book.

Examples of Family-Friendly Policies

For Faculty and Staff

The Duke Child Care Partnership increases the number of high-quality childcare spaces available in the community and provides priority placement for Duke families at participating centers. The program is a unique partnership between Duke and Child Care Services Association (CCSA) to address the lack of childcare. Duke faculty, staff, and students receive priority spaces in participating facilities when they become available. More than 1,000 new four-star and five-star childcare slots have been created as a result, including 168 new infant and toddler spaces, thus addressing the problem in a systemic, sustainable way that benefits not only Duke affiliates but also the wider community.

For more information, visit http://www.hr.duke.edu/dccp/.

The Campus Child Care Homes Network at the University of Michigan is a university-supported network of independent, state-licensed childcare homes. It expands the number of campus-serving childcare spaces beyond university childcare centers and includes evening, weekend, and drop-in care availability for children of all ages.

Network childcare providers offer some enrollment priority to university families and work toward training goals and possible program accreditation through the National Association for Family Child Care (NAFCC). In return, the university provides support including achievement-based financial incentives, small-equipment grants, training opportunities, and paid professional memberships and accreditation fees.

For more information, visit http://hr.umich.edu/worklife/childcare/homesnetwork.php.

liveWELL at the University of Iowa is a comprehensive and proactive health improvement program designed to work with faculty and staff to help them adopt and enhance behaviors that lead to improved health and productivity. With more than a 50% participation rate, liveWELL has shown improvements in population health behaviors and risks for chronic disease. liveWELL has demonstrated cost savings by reducing predicted monthly medical expenditures for individuals who work one-on-one with a personal health coach. A key component of this client-centered program is collaboration with local health care providers and internal resources such as the Employee Assistance Program, Family Services Office, and Career Counseling Service.

For more information, visit http://www.uiowa.edu/livewell.

Working at IOWA (WAI) is a campuswide survey assessing engagement among faculty and staff. WAI seeks to better understand the strengths of the university as an employer, celebrate successes, and continue to commit to the effort of improving the workplace culture. The initial survey occurred in April 2006 with resurveying to occur in October 2008. With the completion of the second survey, information will be available to assess continuous improvement. The hope is to resurvey every 2 to 3 years. Results are reported for the university-wide level and for the division/college level with action plans developed addressing both levels.

For more information, visit http://www.uiowa.edu/hr/working/index .html.

The **UC Faculty Family Friendly Edge** is an initiative designed to develop and implement a comprehensive package of innovative work–family policies and programs for ladder-rank faculty in the UC system. Initiatives include stopping the tenure clock, paid leave, and a flexible part-time appointment for faculty. In addition, the UC programs offers active service modified duties (ASMD) to help faculty reduce normal duties to prepare and/or care for a child.

For more information, visit http://ucfamilyedge.berkeley.edu/uc familyfriendlyedge.html.

University of Kentucky Elder Care is a free employee benefit established to support regular full-time and part-time UK faculty, staff, retirees and their spouses nationwide who help their parents, spouses, and other older family members. The program was established in 1983; staff provide information, consultation, guidance, and referrals to help caregivers plan ahead. When services, equipment, or special-care facilities are needed, referrals are individually researched and mailed within 3 working days to the employee.

For more information, visit http://www.uky.edu/HR/Elder Care/welcome.html.

The **University of Florida's Dual Career Services Program** was established as a program within the provost's office to accommodate new university faculty who are attempting to relocate their partner. Services include job search assistance for up to 1 year, external employer networking (local and regional), access to job openings and career consulting services available at UF, and relocation information and support services (real estate agents, schools, churches, day care, banks, etc.).

For more information, visit http://www.aa.ufl.edu/aa/facdev/support/ dual-career.shtml.

The **Breastfeeding Support Program (BSP)** at the University of California, Davis, provides breastfeeding moms a place to express milk during their work or school day. BSP operates 33 sites on the UC Davis main and Medical Center campuses, all equipped with hospital-grade pumps. New campus design guidelines require that all new construction include lactation rooms. Nine additional sites are expected to open by 2011. As early as 2002, BSP received the Innovative Excellence Award from the Alliance for Work/Life Professionals for creativity and innovation in work–life programming. In 2005, UC Davis was one of three employers statewide to be commended by the California Task Force on Youth and Workplace Wellness for exemplary commitment to family health promotion and lactation accommodation in the workplace.

For more information, visit http://www.hr.ucdavis.edu/Work_Life/Life/ breastfeed/breastfeed.

The **Employee Education Program (EEP) and the Family Education Program (FEP)** at the University of Kentucky provide tuition assistance to employees and their dependents. Tuition discounts are based on years of continuous, full-time university employment and cannot exceed 50% of in-state tuition. To be eligible for the discount, students must be admitted to the University of Kentucky in good academic standing and registered in undergraduate, for-credit classes.

For more information, visit http://www.uky.edu/HR/benefits/eep_fep_overview.html.

Lehigh University Work/Life Balance Research Grants are small ($6,000) one-time grants that are awarded to help untenured faculty members sustain research productivity while caring for a child or other family member. The grants may be used for research purposes, including travel to conferences, computer equipment, research assistance, and other research requirements. In addition, the research grants can be used for expenses related to caring for a child or family member, such as daycare or housekeeping.

For more information, visit http://www.lehigh.edu/~insloan/research grants.html.

For Graduate Students

Princeton University offers six family-focused programs to graduate students: (1) Childbirth Accommodation and Adoption Policy (2) Student Child Care Assistance Program, (3) Work Options Backup Care, (4) Carebridge, (5) Dependent Care Travel Fund, and (6) Mortgage Program. Under the Childbirth Accommodation and Adoption Policy, graduate students who give birth are entitled to 12 weeks of paid maternity leave and all academic obligations are suspended. In addition, birth mothers and all primary caregivers pursuing doctorates are eligible for an extension of academic deadlines that provides one additional term of financial support for each child that enters the home.

For more information about all of Princeton's policies, visit http://grad school.princeton.edu/studentlife/childcare/.

Organizations, Research Centers, and Mailing Lists

The College and University Work/Family Association (CUWFA) provides information and services to all those contributing to the development of work–family programs in higher education, including human resources administrators, student services administrators, work–family managers, senior administrators, faculty, and others.

For more information, visit http://www.cuwfa.org.

American Association of University Professors (AAUP) Statement of Principles on Family Responsibilities and Academic Work. This is the official statement of the AAUP on issues related to faculty career flexibility. Among its highlights are the suggestion that relief be provided for probationary faculty who experience the arrival of a new child in the home.

For the entire statement, visit http://www.aaup.org/AAUP/pubsres/policy docs/contents/workfam-stmt.htm.

The Work/Family Newsgroup is a weekly moderated e-mail discussion group for scholars, practitioners, and others interested in work–family balance issues. Announcements include advertisements of upcoming conferences, recent publications, and national and state legislation.

To join, send an e-mail to drago@psu.edu with your e-mail address.

The Berkeley Parents Network (BPN) is a parent-run e-mail forum for more than 20,000 parents who live in the Berkeley, California, area. Founded in 1993 by graduate students at UC Berkeley, the list has since been expanded to include all interested parents in the nearby communities. BPN gives busy parents an easy way to help and support each other by posting a message to one of the newsletters. Members can ask questions about parenting, give advice to other parents, find out about local resources and community events, look for childcare, sell household items, and more.

For more information, visit http://parents.berkeley.edu.

Mama PhD is a blog sponsored by insidehighered.com that catalogs the insights and experiences of several academic mothers.

To access the blog, visit http://www.insidehighered.com/views/blogs/mama_phd.

The **Families and Work Institute** is a nonprofit center that conducts research on the changing workforce, the changing workplace, and the changing family. The institute's research centers on four main topical areas: (1) the workforce and workplace, (2) education, care, and community, (3) parenting, and (4) youth development.

For more information, visit http://www.familiesandwork.org.

The **Center for Work & Family** at Boston College helps organizations create workplaces that support and develop healthy and productive employees. The center has two primary missions. First, it focuses on bridging academic research and corporate practice; second, it focuses on the need for cultural change.

For more information, visit http://www.bc.edu/centers/cwf/.

Reports, Articles, and Books

The National Clearinghouse on Academic Worklife (NCAW) is a resource that brings together articles, research and policy reports, policies, demographics, additional Web sites, and narratives on institutional policy change. Hosted by the Center for the Education of Women at the University of Michigan, NCAW provides resources to help scholars and administrators understand more about academic work–family issues.

For more information, visit http://www.academicworklife.org.

An Agenda for Excellence: Creating Flexibility in Tenure-Track Faculty Careers is the first product of a grant to ACE from the Alfred P. Sloan Foundation to fund the project Creating Options: Models for Flexible Tenure-Track Career Pathways. Outlined in the report are the specific project goals.

For more information, visit http://www.acenet.edu/AM/Template.cfm? Section = Home&TEMPLATE = /CM/ContentDisplay.cfm&CONTENTID = 20910.

Beyond Bias and Barriers: Fulfilling the Potential of Women in Academic Science and Engineering is a comprehensive book that outlines the findings of a national meeting of recognized experts on topics such as recent developments in employment discrimination law and programs and strategies used by universities and other employers to advance the careers of female scientists and engineers.

For more information, visit http://books.nap.edu/openbook.php?isbn = 0309100429.

Workplace Flexibility: Innovation in Action is an e-book released by WorldatWork, an association of human resources professionals that focuses on attracting and retaining employees. The book is an outcome of a September 2007 retreat hosted by the Alliance for Work–Life Progress and funded by the Alfred P. Sloan Foundation that brought together representatives from higher education and corporate leaders in work–life flexibility. The book offers tips on how to redesign organizational culture to encourage and promote workplace flexibility.

For more information, visit http://www.worldatwork.org/mypeers/ebook/ WorkplaceFlexBook2_08.pdf.

Rethinking Faculty Work: Higher Education's Strategic Imperative explores how changes in higher education are transforming the careers of faculty and provides a model that makes it possible for all faculty to be in a position to do their best. This important resource offers a vision of academic workplaces that will attract superb faculty committed to fulfilling the missions of the universities and colleges where they work.

For more information, visit http://www.josseybass.com/WileyCDA/ WileyTitle/productCd-078796613 4.html.

Transforming Science and Engineering: Advancing Academic Women reports the results of institutions that received the National Science Foundation's ADVANCE grants to improve the climate for women in science and engineering. The book highlights various strategies that may be effective at different institutions across the country.

For more information, visit http://www.press.umich.edu/titleDetail Desc.do;jsessionid=A23B7F42DE0D28E886CCE984D7DA9E71?id=178866.

ABOUT THE AUTHORS

Emily Arms brings 20 years of professional experience in the field of education to her research and writing on gender. Currently an independent research consultant, she has served on the faculties of the University of Southern California, Loyola Marymount University, and UCLA, where she earned her Ph.D. in 2002. Her most recent publication, co-authored with Dr. Linda Sax, is "Gender Differences Over the Span of College: Challenges to Achieving Equity" in the *Journal About Women in Higher Education.*

Kathleen Beauchesne is the former director of the Faculty and Staff Assistance Program (FASAP), the Student Assistance Program for medical and graduate students, the School of Medicine, and the Bloomberg School of Public Health and WORKlife Programs at the Johns Hopkins Institutions (JHI). She is a nationally recognized expert with capabilities in positioning, developing, leading, and managing behavioral health, employee and student assistance, work–life and workforce effectiveness programs, and policies in complex environments. She ran one of the largest internal integrated employee and student assistance and work–life programs serving 40,000 faculty, staff and employees of JHI, and 3,500 students. After 20 years at Hopkins, Beauchesne retired at the end of January 2007 and now maintains an active consulting practice. She was the first recipient of the EAPA President's Award in 2004. She is currently the human resources officer for the board of directors for the Maryland Committee for Children. She is a founding member of the College and University Work and Family Association and the Work and Family Network of Maryland, the founding chair of the national Work and Family Committee of the Employee Assistance Professional Association (EAPA), and a past member of the board of directors for the Alliance of WorkLife Progress.

Jill Bickett is a career education professional. After receiving her M.A. in English from Loyola Marymount University, she began a 23-year teaching career at Marymount High School in Los Angeles that included leadership positions as English department chairperson, academic dean, and assistant head. She received her Ed.D. from the University of Southern California. Recent work includes her dissertation, *A Case Study of Leadership and Service in a Catholic Single-Sex High School,* and a co-authored article, "Gender Bias and Imbalance: The Underrepresentation of Girls in Special Education," published in the international journal *Gender and Education* (2008).

Sharon Dannels is an associate professor at George Washington University and coordinator of the Educational Research Methods faculty. Her Ph.D. is in experimental psychology, although her background includes training and experience as an outpatient mental health therapist as well as a postdoctorate in internal medicine. Her research spans such areas as the biological basis of personality, the effect of prophylactic drugs on cognitive processes, individual differences in workload assessment, physiological correlates of obesity, the efficacy of distance education, and women and leadership. Before coming to George Washington University, she taught for the University of Maryland in Okinawa, Japan. She currently teaches doctoral courses in both qualitative and quantitative research methods.

Mariko Dawson Zare is a Ph.D. candidate in English at the University of Southern California. Her years of service on the Graduate and Professional Student Senate Women's Concerns Committee also include a year as committee chair. Her experience as a graduate student and a parent has been useful in the committee's work toward making USC a family-friendly campus, which has resulted in a graduate student parental leave program, lactation facilities, and fostering a support network for graduate student parents. In an effort to further represent the needs of both graduate students and their families, she also served as graduate student representative on the university's student health insurance committee as an advocate for better coverage for graduate students and their dependents. Her experience with work–life balance in an academic context began as an undergraduate at the University of California, Los Angeles, where she completed her B.A. in English while working full-time in various fields, including the hotel industry, legal marketing, and a medical testing corporation.

Karie Frasch is an academic researcher at the University of California, Berkeley, focusing on gender equity issues in higher education. Before she worked there, her research concentrated on children and families involved with the child welfare system. She received her Ph.D. in social welfare from UC Berkeley in 2001. She is currently the manager of the UC Faculty Family Friendly Edge, a series of projects and initiatives designed to develop and implement a comprehensive package of innovative work–family policies and programs for ladder-rank faculty in the UC system. As part of one of these projects, UC Berkeley's Alfred P. Sloan Foundation Award for Faculty Career Flexibility, she authored *Creating a Family Friendly Department: Chairs and Deans Toolkit.* Another project, Federal Grants and the Academic Pipeline, explores the role of federal funding in the academic careers of graduate students, postdoctoral fellows, soft-money researchers, and faculty.

Marc Goulden studies work, family, and equity issues among academics. He has a Ph.D. from the University of Wisconsin, Madison (1995), with a focus on the diversity and life course of students and faculty in college and university settings. His recent work has been with Mary Ann Mason on the "Do Babies Matter?" project. Using data from the Survey of Doctorate Recipients, Mason and Goulden have examined the relationship between gender, family, and career outcomes and the effect of academic careers on family outcomes among male and female Ph.D.s. The project has resulted in a number of papers that have received considerable attention, and the *Chronicle of Higher Education* recently profiled Goulden as one of Higher Education's Next Generation of Thinkers. Goulden's current research agenda also includes two Alfred P. Sloan Foundation–funded projects: The UC Faculty Family Friendly Edge and Federal Grants and the Academic Pipeline (see http://ucfamilyedge.berkeley.edu). The first project involves the development of a set of systemwide family-friendly policy and program recommendations aimed at giving the University of California a competitive advantage. The second explores the role of federal funding in the academic careers of graduate students, postdoctoral fellows, soft-money researchers, and faculty.

Jeni Hart is an assistant professor for the Department of Educational Leadership and Policy Analysis at the University of Missouri–Columbia. Her scholarship centers on two mutually reinforcing themes: academic work and campus–work life climate. She has examined how feminism influences academic work, particularly in research and service. One aspect of faculty service central to her agenda is feminist faculty activism. She conceptualized two different types of feminist faculty activists: professionalized activists and activist professionals. In addition, she has considered myriad strategies activists use, including how, with whom, and why they create networks to advance their activist agendas. She is also Co–Principal Investigator on an NSF ADVANCE grant intended to develop and sustain data-driven programs that enhance the work environment for associate and full female faculty in science, technology, engineering, and mathematics (STEM). Hart completed her B.S. in foreign service at Georgetown University, her M.Ed. in higher education and student affairs administration at the University of Vermont, and her Ph.D. in higher education administration at the University of Arizona. She worked for 9 years as a student affairs educator at a number of colleges and universities, and 1 year as a faculty member at Southeast Missouri State University before joining the faculty at the University of Missouri.

Caryn Jung is senior coordinator for UA Life & Work Connections' child and elder care and work–life programs at the University of Arizona. She has served as a business consultant and a national, regional, and local presenter on workplace initiatives. She holds an M.S. degree with a concentration in work–life, family care, and gerontological issues from the University of Arizona and an undergraduate degree in child development. Jung also serves as vice president of the College and University Work/Family Association (CUWFA).

Jaime Lester is assistant professor of higher education at George Mason University. Lester holds a Ph.D. and an M.Ed. in higher education from the Rossier School of Education at the University of Southern California. Before joining George Mason University, she was an assistant professor and co-director of the Research Center for Community College Inquiry in the Department of Leadership and Counseling at Old Dominion University from 2006 to 2008. Lester maintains an active research agenda that examines gender equity in higher education; retention and transfer of community college students; socialization of women and minority faculty; and leadership. She has published articles in the *Community College Journal of Research and Practice, Community College Review, Journal of Higher Education, Liberal Education, National Women's Studies Association Journal,* and *NEA:*

Thought & Action. She also has written several forthcoming books on gendered perspectives in community colleges and ways to restructure higher education to promote collaboration.

Sharon A. McDade is director of the American Council on Education Fellows Program while on professional leave from a faculty position with the higher education administration graduate program at George Washington University. Previously she was a faculty member at Teachers College/Columbia University and director of the Institute for Educational Management Programs at Harvard University. She has served as external evaluator for the Hedwig van Ameringen Executive Leadership in Academic Medicine (ELAM) program (based at Drexel University) for more than a decade. This research was most recently sponsored by a 5-year grant from the Robert Wood Johnson Foundation. Her research, teaching, and consulting has focused on the leadership development of higher education administrators as well as the management of colleges and universities. She has developed leadership programs for and worked with senior administrators of higher education and business in the United States and abroad. She served on the board of directors of the American Association for Higher Education from 1988 to 1992. Her degrees include an Ed.D. in administration, planning, and social policy from Harvard University's Graduate School of Education, an M.F.A. in design and theater technology from Ohio State University, and a B.S. from Miami University.

Jean McLaughlin is a research associate at the American Council on Education, where she works on the Alfred P. Sloan projects for faculty career flexibility. McLaughlin also has researched career issues for women in academic medicine. Before becoming a doctoral candidate in higher education administration at George Washington University, she was a career counselor for business students. She has a master's degree in counseling and personnel services from the University of Maryland and a bachelor's degree in art history from the Catholic University of America.

Mary Ann Mason is professor of the Graduate School and co-director of the Berkeley Law Center on Health, Economic & Family Security (CHEFS) at the University of California, Berkeley. From 2000 to 2007, she served as the first female dean of the Graduate Division at UC Berkeley, with responsibility for nearly 10,000 students in more than 100 graduate programs. During her tenure, she championed diversity in the graduate student population, promoted equity for student parents, and pioneered measures to enhance work–life balance for all faculty. Her research findings and advocacy have been central to groundbreaking policy initiatives, including the 10-campus UC Faculty Family Friendly Edge and the nationwide Nine Presidents summits on gender equity at major research universities. Her most recent book (co-authored with her daughter, Eve Mason Ekman) is *Mothers on the Fast Track: How a New Generation Can Balance Family and Careers.*

Sharon Page-Medrich is an academic analyst at the University of California, Berkeley, supporting the dean of the graduate division as well as the campus's initiatives for diversity and equity. In addition, since 2002 she has assisted the research and dissemination efforts of the "Do Babies Matter?" project, the UC Faculty Family Friendly Edge initiative, and related projects focused on gender, family, work, academia, and public policy. She is a graduate of Mills College.

Kate Quinn is project director for Balance@UW, an Alfred P. Sloan Foundation–funded initiative to increase the flexibility of faculty careers at the University of Washington. Her research focuses on the ways in which higher education policy, climate/culture, and leadership interact to structure work–life balance for faculty and students. She is the recipient of the 2008 Society of Women Engineers Work Life Balance Award, which "celebrates an individual who has worked to create programs that help women engineers and other employees balance the commitments of career, life and family." She has presented research findings and policy recommendations nationally and is published in *Academe* and *Change.* Additionally, she has articles forthcoming in the *Journal of the Professoriate,* the *Journal About Women in Higher Education,* and *The Department Chair.* A nationally recognized expert in the field of work–life flexibility in higher education, she receives numerous invitations to participate in national meetings and to present at conferences. She received her Ph.D. in educational leadership and policy studies from the University of Washington.

Margaret Sallee is assistant professor of higher education in the Department of Educational Leadership and Policy Studies at The University of Tennessee. Her research interests focus on two broad areas: academic work and the student experience. With academic work, she explores the nature of faculty work and the steps that institutions take to create and sustain diverse faculties. As part of that work, she also focuses on issues of work–family balance within higher education. With student experience, she brings a gender lens to the experiences of graduate students. Her most recent study investigated the experiences of male graduate students in two disciplines, considering the relationship between socialization, discipline, and masculinities. Before joining the faculty at the University of Tennessee, she earned her Ph.D. in urban education with an emphasis on higher education from the University of Southern California. While at USC, she advocated for family-friendly policies on campus. Through her work as chair of a campus committee formed to address the needs of graduate students, she was part of a successful multi-year effort to implement family and medical leave for graduate students, served on a committee that created two lactation rooms, and began a support group for graduate student parents.

Randi Shapiro is assistant director of Benefits & Work/Life at the University of Washington. With more than 20 years of experience in the work–life field in higher education, Shapiro has a proven track record for innovative program development and building collaboration throughout the institution. Under her leadership, UW won several family-friendly awards and grants, including a Washington State Child Care Advantage award in 1991 and the Breastfeeding Coalition of Washington State Outstanding Employer Award in 2006. Additionally, Shapiro secured for UW more than $1.5 million in competitive state and federal grants for childcare center facility development and expansion (i.e., capital) and tuition subsidy support for students. In addition to oversight of work–life, dependent-care, lactation support, employee assistance, and discount programs, Shapiro is responsible for developing and implementing a university-wide recognition program. Within a 3-month period she rolled out recognition training to more than 500 managers and supervisors as part of a culture change initiative. A founding member of the College and University Work/Family Association (CUWFA), she is a leader in work–life in higher education and a frequent presenter at national conferences.

David L. Swihart is employee assistance coordinator for Life & Work Connections at the University of Arizona. He is a licensed professional counselor and is a member of the International Employee Assistance Professionals in Education.

Gloria D. Thomas was appointed executive director of the Center for the Education of Women (CEW) at the University of Michigan on January 1, 2009. CEW provides counseling and educational programs regarding academic, career, and life issues; conducts social research on policy and gender issues; and advocates for improved policy and practice. Previously, she served in various positions at the American Council on Education (ACE) for nearly 8 years, including associate director of the Office of Women in Higher Education, associate project director of the Center for Effective Leadership/Sloan Projects, and associate director of the ACE Fellows Program, all where the foci of her professional duties were leadership development and enhancing career success for women in academe. Before ACE, she worked at CEW conducting research and coordinating the Women of Color in the Academy project, a support network for faculty women of color at the University of Michigan. She also served as associate dean of admissions and director of minority student recruitment at Swarthmore College. She holds a B.A. in English and Black studies from Swarthmore College, an M.A. in English from Villanova University, and a Ph.D. in higher education from the University of Michigan.

Darci A. Thompson is director of Life & Work Connections at the University of Arizona. Her primary work includes the strategic direction of the unit, supervisory and administrative consultation, and collaborative work with other campus entities to continue to improve family friendliness at the UA. Thompson has presented to national, state, and local forums. She serves as an external consultant/educator, research associate, and faculty associate of the Arizona State University School of Social Work.

INDEX